I0024148

Alexander Wood Inglis

The vocal magazine

Containing a selection of the most esteemed English, Scots, and Irish songs. Vol. 1

Alexander Wood Inglis

The vocal magazine
Containing a selection of the most esteemed English, Scots, and Irish songs. Vol. 1

ISBN/EAN: 9783337126346

Printed in Europe, USA, Canada, Australia, Japan

Cover: Foto ©Thomas Meinert / pixelio.de

More available books at **www.hansebooks.com**

THE

VOCAL MAGAZINE.

CONTAINING

A SELECTION

OF

THE MOST ESTEEMED

ENGLISH, SCOTS, AND IRISH SONGS,

ANTIENT AND MODERN:

ADAPTED FOR THE HARPSICHORD OR VIOLIN.

VOL. I.

O decus Phœbi, et dapibus supremi
Grata testudo Jovis, o laborum
Dulce lenimen!　　　HOR.

Edinburgh:

PRINTED BY C. STEWART & CO.

1797.

[PRICE—10 s. 6 d. bound.]

TO

MISS HENRIETTA HUNTER,

THIS VOLUME

OF

THE VOCAL MAGAZINE,

WHICH HAS BEEN HONOURED WITH THE APPROBATION

OF ONE WHO IS SO EMINENTLY QUALIFIED

TO JUDGE OF ITS MERIT,

IS RESPECTFULLY INSCRIBED,

BY

THE EDITORS.

ADVERTISEMENT.

AMONG the relaxations from the fatigues and bufinefs of life, there are none more innocent or more delightful than Mufic. Among the accomplifhments of modern education, and particularly that of the fair fex, none are more elegant or more attractive, and confequently none more juftly fafhionable than fkill in the practice of Mufic, whether vocal or inftrumental. But befides the expence which attends the acquifition of that fkill, the purchafe of engraved Mufic and the choice and felection of proper pieces are obftacles in the way of many performers, efpecially of fuch as live in the country or at a diftance from the advice of perfons of tafte.

On confidering the ftate of Vocal Mufic, it appeared to the Editors that there was wanting in this country, fome felect collection, at a cheap rate, of antient and modern Songs, with claffical and appropriate words. Of fingle fongs there are in the Mufic fhops a very great number ; but comparatively few of real and approved merit. A fet of thefe, even though chofen with care and tafte, cannot be had uniform ; and the expence is confiderable. Our modern compofers are very indifferent as to the choice of words ; which are often infignificant, and fometimes abfurd. The engravers of mufic are generally illiterate, and where the correctnefs is left to them, which feems to be too often the cafe, the errors we find in their works often acquire a currency among thofe whofe education is imperfect.

The object therefore of this publication is to remedy as much as poffible thefe inconveniencies. A felect collection of good Mufic, with words by the beft Englifh Authors, is they believe, no where elfe to be found. Some works fimilar to the following, fuch as the Mufical Mifcellany, met with very great fuccefs and are now grown fcarce. Thefe, however, are all inferior, in point of execution at leaft, to the Vocal Magazine ; while the invention of printing the Mufic with moveable types enables the Editors to afford it at a price infinitely below that of engraved Mufic.

With regard to the felection, they have endeavoured to give variety, that the tafte of different people might be gratified. They hope, that though in a collection every piece cannot be of equal merit, yet that they have admitted none which

will

will not pleafe judges. The words are chofen from the works of the beft authors ; and they hope they have avoided every thing that can give offence even to
the moft delicate.

In this northern part of our ifland, vocal harmony, it muft be confeffed, is but
little cultivated ; moft young ladies contenting themfelves with finging alone or
with a harpfichord accompaniment, but few attempting to fing in parts. Of late
indeed, among fome of the beft fingers, attempts have been made to introduce the
practice, and it is now becoming fashionable. To encourage this tafte, a few of the
moft favourite duos and trios, have been inferted in the following volume, which,
it is hoped, may be ufeful in removing from our fair countrywomen, the reproach
of being behind their fouthern neighbours in fo elegant an accomplifhment.

CONTENTS.

	WORDS.	MUSIC.	SONG.
A			
At dead of night the hour when courts	Rev. Mr Cameron.	Pleyel.	5
A fig for the cares of this whirligig world	Col. Fitzpatrick.	Irish.	14
Ah where can fly my foul's true love	-	Pleyel.	26
A shepherd once had lost his love	-	Storace.	29
A sup of good whisky will make you glad	-	-	33
A poor little gipsey	-	-	57
Ah! tell me why should silly man	-	Storace.	63
All in the downs	Gay.	Leveridge.	94
As o'er the heath	Aiken.	Sheels.	106
As Kate one morn	-	Dr Arnold.	110
At dead of night when care gives place	-	-	115
Adieu the verdant lawns	-	-	116
B			
Brisk wine and lovely women	-	Dr Arnold.	12
Bow the head, thou lily fair	Aiken.	Haydn.	21
Behold the fatal hour arrive	Lord Hales.	Irish.	23
Bright Phebus has mounted	-	-	31
Beneath this green willow	-	Schulz.	79
Blow ye bleak winds	-	Arne.	84
C			
Come pull away, boys	-	-	19
Could you to battle march away	-	-	41
Come live with me	Marlow.	Webbe.	55
Coming o'er the craigs o' Kyle	-	-	58
Come buy of poor Kate	-	-	64
Come all ye souls devoid of art	-	-	76
Come let's be merry	-	-	100
Come my pretty love	-	-	108
Cottage boy	-	-	114
D			
Declare ye banks of Helicon	-	-	10
E			
Enrolled in our bright annals lives	Lord Mornington.	Zelter.	89
F			
From night to morn I take my glafs	-	-	41
For ever fortune	-	Jackson.	73
From grave lessons	-	Weldon.	81
For tenderness form'd	Gen. Buagoyne.	-	93
G			
Gin a body meet a body	-	-	53
H			
Ho! why dost thou shiver and shake	Altered from Holcroft. Mr S. Clark		6
Here awa Willie	-	-	13

	WORDS.	MUSIC.	SONG.
Happy the man who lifes' dull cares	-	-	40
Hail flow'ry meads -	-		54
How long and dreary is the night	-	-	61
Hail ! hail green fields -		-	62
Haste my Nanette - -	Prior.	Travers.	82
How pleased within my native bow'rs	Shenstone,	Shield.	88
How stands the glass around	-	Handel.	101
Hang my lyre upon the willow	Lovebond.	-	109
Hey ho ! to the green wood	-	-	117

I

John Anderson my jo, John	Burns.	-	27
In the dark and lonely bow'r	-	-	37
In the dead of the night -	-	-	39
In vain I try my every art	-	-	50
If love and all the world were young	Raleigh.	S. Webbe.	56
In my pleasant native plains -			72
I pass all my hours - -	-		72
I pass all my hours - -	Charles II.	Humphrey.	75
If the treasur'd gold could give -	Anacreon.	Reichardt.	83
I am a poor shepherd undone -			96
I am, cry'd Apollo - -	Fontaine.		107

K

Kind Robin lo'es me -	-		76

L

Life has no real bliss in store	Mrs H. Pye.	French air.	28
Let us all be unhappy together			70
Little thinks the town's-mans wife			103
Love's a triffling silly passion	-	Monro.	104

M

My love she's but a lassie yet			5
My days have been so wond'rous free			86
Milkmaid - -	-	Arnold.	110
Morn shakes her locks -			114

N

Non nobis Domine -		Byrd.	22
Night to lovers joys a friend		Tarsi.	46
Now westlin winds - -	Burns.	Reichardt.	78

O

O listen to the voice of love	-	Hook.	4
O see that form that faintly gleams			9
O sing unto my roundelay -	Chatterton.	Paxton.	24
O wat ye wha's in yon town	Burns.		25
O I hae seen the roses blaw -	Hamilton.	Muschet.	35
Of all the girls that are so smart		Carey.	44
Oh ! the moment was sad -			65
O ye in youth and beauty's pride	-	Schulz	91
O Venus, beauty of the skies	Sappho.	Schulz.	92
O where have ye been a' day	Capt. M'Niel.		105

P

Poll dang it how d'ye do -	-		38

R

Remember O thou man -	-		8

(3)

	WORDS.	MUSIC:	SONG.
Roy's wife of Aldivalloch	-		97
S			
Sigh no more ladies - -	Percy.	Stevens.	34
Stay, traveller, tarry here to-night	-	Linley. .	47
Sir Eglamore was a valiant knight	-	-	51
She came from the hills of the weft	-	Irifh.	59
Say ye ftudious, grave and old -		-	60
Savourna Delifh -			65
Since I'm born a mortal man -			69
Since Emma caught -	•	Travers.	77
Sappho's Ode -	-		92
Some women take delight in drefs	-	-	95
Sweet Sir for your courtefy -		•	113
T			
Thou to whofe eyes I bend	-	W.Jackfon.	1
The king fits in Dunfermline town	-	-	11
Take, oh take thofe lips away	Johnfon.	Smith.	15
'Twas near a thicket's calm retreat	Moulds.	-	17
Tibbie Fowler o' the glen	-	-	36
Tell me thou dear departed fhade	-	-	42
To dear Amaryllis -	Mendez.	French.	45
Thou dear feducer of my heart	-	Fifher.	49
To fair Fidele's graffy tomb -	Collins.	Arne.	52
'Tis not wealth -	-	Gardini.	80
There's nought but care on ev'ry hand	Burns.		85
To Anacreon in heaven -		-	87
The lover how bleft -	-	Schulz.	98
The night when fpent -		Shield.	102
Tafte life's glad moments	-	German.	111
V			
Vain is ev'ry fond endeavour -	-	Boyce.	99
W			
Why fteals from my bofom the figh	Mr M'Kenzie.	Ebden.	2
When father Adam firft did flee	-	-	7
We be three poor mariners -			18
We be foldiers three -	•	-	30
Were I oblig'd to beg my bread	-	-	48
When youth's fprightly flood	-	Arne.	66
Where the bee fucks -	-	Arne.	67
What bleft hours untainted by forrow	-	Linley.	68
We bipeds made up of frail clay	-	-	70
When youth his fairy reign began	-	Arne.	71
While I quaff the rofy wine •		-	74
Wilt thou be my dearie -	Burns.	:	90
When Nicholas firft to court began			112
Y			
Ye birds for whom I rear'd the grove	Shenftone.		32
Ye banks and braes of bonny Down	Burns.	Mr Millar.	43

The
Vocal Magazine.

Vol. I.

INVOCATION.

BY WILLIAM JACKSON

Larghetto. Pia.

Thou to whose eyes I bend, Thou to whose eyes I bend,

Thou to whose eyes I bend

Forte   *Pia*

at whose command (tho' low my voice tho' artless be my hand)

at whose command (tho' low my voice tho' artless be my hand)

Allegro. Forte

I take the sprightly reed and sing or play, careless of all

I take the sprightly reed and sing or play, careless of all

care-less of all care-less of all the cens-ring world may say

careless of all careless of all the cens'ring world may say

I take the fprightly reed and fing or play, carelefs of all the

I take the fprightly reed and fing or play carelefs of

Crescendo il forte.

cens'- ring world . the cens'- ring world may fay I

all the cens'ring world may fay I take the fpri ghtly

Mezzo forte

take the fprightly reed and fing and fing or play I take the fprightly

reed the fprightly reed and fing or play,

reed and fing or play; I take the fprightly reed the

and fing or play, I take the fprightly reed I take the fprightly

fprightly reed & play

reed the fprightly reed & play & fing or play carelefs of

Larghetto

carelefs of all the cens'ring world may fay   O   fairest of thy fex! O faireft

all   all the cens'ring world may fay.   O   faireft of thy fex!   O faireft

of thy fex   be thou my Mufe,   deign on my   work thy influence to dif- fufe

of thy fex be thou my Mufe,   deign on my   work thy iufluence to dif- fufe

Allegro Forte

fo fhall my notes to   future   times to future   times pro- claim unbounded

fo fhall my notes to future   times to   future   times pro- claim unbounded

love and e- ver   during flame; fo fhall my notes proclaim unbounded   love

love and e- ver   during flame;   fo fhall my notes proclaim unbounded

fo fhall my notes proclaim   unbound- ed   love un- bounded   love

love;   fo fhall my   notes   pro - claim unbound- ed   love,   fo

CONTINUED,

proclaim unbounded love and e- ver dur- ing flame so
shall my notes proclaim unbound- ed love and e- ver during flame;
shall my notes proclaim unbounded love so shall my
unbounded love so shall my notes proclaim
notes proclaim pro- claim unbound- ed love
so shall my notes proclaim proclaim unbounded love un-
un- bounded love and
bounded love unbounded love and ever
e- ver during flame.
e- ver during flame.

SONG II.

WHY STEALS FROM MY BOSOM.

Why steals from my bo - som the sigh? Why

Why steals from my bo - som the sigh? Why

fix'd is my gaze on the ground? Come give me my

fix'd is my gaze on the ground? Come give me my

Pipe and I'll try To banish my cares with the

Pipe and I'll try To banish my cares with the

found. 'Twas taught by La - vi - nia's sweet smile, In

found. 'Twas taught by La - vi - nia's sweet smile, In

the mirth- lov- ing cho- rus to join; Ah me! how un-

the mirth-lov- ing cho- rus to join; Ah me! how un-

weet - ing the while, La - vi - nia can ne -

weeting the while, La- vi - nia can ne -

ver be mine.

ver be mine.

II.

I lean on my hand with a ſigh;
  My friends the ſoft ſadneſs condemn;
Yet methinks, tho' I cannot tell why,
  I ſhould hate to be merry like them.

When I walk'd in the pride of the dawn
  Methought all the region look'd bright :
Has fweetnefs forfaken the lawn ?
  For methinks, I grow fad at the fight.

III.

Let me walk where the foft-rifing wave
  Has pictur'd the moon on its breaft ;
Let me walk where the new cover'd grave
  Allows the pale lover to reft !

When fhall I in its peaceable tomb,
  Be laid with my forrows afleep !
Should Lavinia but chance on my tomb
  I could die if I thought fhe would weep.

SONG III.

MY LOVE IS BUT A LASSIE YET.

My Love fhe's but a Las - sie yet, My Love fhe's but a

Las - sie yet, We'll let her ftand a year or twa fhe'll no be

half fae fau - cy yet. I rue the day I fought her

O I rue the day I fought her O, Wha gets her need na

fay he's woo'd But he may fay he's bought her O.

SONG IV.

LISTEN TO THE VOICE OF LOVE.

Music by HOOK

Andantino

O liſt-en liſt-en to the voice of

Love, He calls my Daph-ne to the grove; The

Prim - rose sweet be - decks the field, The tune - ful birds in - vite to rove To soft - er joys let splen - dor yield, O list-en list-en to - - - the voice of Love.

Where flow'rs their blooming sweets exhale,
My Daphne, let us fondly stray,
Where whisp'ring love breathes forth his tale,
And shepherds sing their artless lay,
O listen to the voice of Love,
He calls my Daphne to the grove.

SONG V.

ROSLIN RUINS.
PLEYEL.

At dead of night, the hour when

courts thro' the wild maze of pleasure rove, And Mira joins th' in - fuar - ing

sports, While art as-sumes the voice of love; To Roslin's ru - ins

I re - pair, a so - li - ta - ry wretch for - lorn, To mourn un -

seen un - pi - tied there my hap -lefs love her cru - el fcorn.

No found of joy difturbs my ftrain,
   No hind is whiftling on the hill;
No herdfman winding o'er the plain,
   No maiden finging by the rill.
Efk, murm'ring thro' the darkfome pines,
   Reflects the moon's uncertain beams;
While thro' the clouds fhe faintly fhines,
   In fancy's eye the pale ghoft gleams.

Not fo the night that in thy halls
   Once, Roslin! danc'd in joy along;
The owl now fcreams within thy walls,
   That echoed mirth's infpiring fong.
Where bats now flit on dufky wings,
   Th' empurpled feaft was wont to flow;
And beauty danc'd in graceful rings,
   Where now the dank weeds baleful grow.

What now avails how great! how gay!
   How fair! how fine, their matchlefs dames
Here sleeps their undiftinguifh'd clay;
   The ftone effac'd has loft their names.
And yon gay crowds muft soon expire,
   Unknown, unprais'd, their fair one's name;
Not so the charms that verfe infpire,
   Increafing years increafe their fame.

Ho! why dost thou shi - ver and shake Gaffer Gray, and

why doth thy nose look so blue? Ho! why dost thou

shi - ver and shake Gaffer Gray, and why doth thy nose look so

blue? 'Tis the weather is cold, and I'm ve - ry old,

and my dou - blet is not ve - ry new Well - a - day! And my

Slower

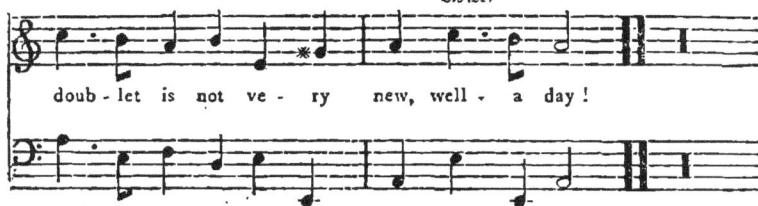

doub - let is not ve - ry new, well - a day !

Then line thy worn doublet with ale , Gaffer Gray !
And warm thy old heart with a glass .
  " Nay , but money I've none ,
  " And my credit's all gone ,
"Then say how may that come to pafs ? Welladay !

Hie away to the houfe on the brow , Gaffer Gray !
And knock at the jolly Priest's door .
  "He has often fupplied me ,
  "And never denied me ;
"But — I dare not go there any more ; Welladay !

The Lawyer lives under the hill , Gaffer Gray !
For candour and juftice rever'd ;
  "He will faften his locks ,
  " And hint that the ftocks ,
"For vagrants and rogues are prepar'd ; Welladay !

The Squire has fat beeves and brown ale , Gaffer Gray ?
And the feason will open his ftore ,
  "His fat beeves and his beer ,
  "And bis merry new year ,
"Are all for the honeft tho' poor ; Welladay !

The wicked and idle in youth ,Gaffer Gray !
Muft expect to be poor when they're old .
  "Alas 'tis my fate ,
  "To feel when too late ,
"The truth I have ever been told ; Welladay !

The Music by Mr. Stephen Clarke , of Edinburgh ; and the Words ,
with a few alterations , by Holcroft .

SONG VII.

FATHER ADAM.

When father Adam first did flee From presence of the Lord his face; Stay Adam, Stay Adam; saith the Lord; Where art thou Adam? turn thee and stay. Who hath reveal'd to thee that naked thou shoudst be; Or hast thou eaten of the tree Which I commanded thee

it touch-ed fhould not be Therefore be - gin - neth thy

mi - fe - ry ; O A - dam poor A-dam I pi - ty thee

☞ This and the following Song are given as fpecimens of old Mufic. They are extracted from a Song-book publifhed at Aberdeen by one Forbes, in the year 1682 intitled Songs and Fancies. It contains, fifty-five Songs, with the Mufic ; or fimple air alone, without bafs or other accompaniment. It is remarkable, that in this collection, there is not one of thofe commonly known at prefent by the name of Scots tunes. The words according to the tafte of the times, are in general on religious fubjects, and often abfurd enough, as appears by the firft verfe of the above Song, which is to be fung as follows ; the words in italics, being ufed at the repeats.

> When Father Adam firft did flee,
> From prefence of the Lord his face,
> *His cloaths was fhort, fcarce cover'd his knee,*
> *The great God cry'd, and held him in chace.*
> Stay Adam, ftay Adam, faith the Lord
> Where art thou Adam ? turn thee and ftay :
> *I was afraid to hear thy voice,*
> *And naked thus to come in thy way :*
> Who hath reveal'd &c.

In the Gentleman's Magazine about two years ago, an inveftigation took place concerning the author of the popular air of God fave the King, and at laft in the Magazine for July 1795, it was finally afcribed (on the authority of one Smith a Mufician at Bath) to Henry Carey, the author of Sally in our Ally, Chrononhotonthologos &c. who had come to Smith with the air to have it harmonized. The refemblance in the 2d ftrain of the following fong, to that of God fave the King, is fo ftriking that we thought our giving it here, might gratify the curious, and perhaps enable them to judge of Carey's title to be thought the author.

The bafses we have added, as we fhall hereafter do to any other we may occafionally felect from the fame, or fimilar works.

C

SONG VIII.

REMEMBER O THOU MAN.

Re - mem- ber O thou man , O thou man , O thou man ;

Re - member O thou man , thy time is fpent. Re - mem- ber

O thou man, how thou waft dead and gone and I did

what I can there- fore re - pent.

Remember Adam's fall, O thou man, O thou man,
Remember Adam's fall from heaven to hell.
Remember Adam's fall, how we were condemned all,
In hell perpetual therein to dwell. &c. &c.

O! fee that form that faint-ly gleams! 'Tis Of-car come to chear my dreams;— On wings of wind he flies a-way; O stay, my love-ly Of-car ftay!

Wake, Ofsian! laft of Fingal's line,
And mix thy tears and fighs with mine;
Awake the harp to doleful lays,
And footh my foul with Ofcar's praise.

The fhell is ceas'd in Ofcar's hall,
Since gloomy Cairbar wrought his fall;
The roe on Morven lightly bounds,
Nor heais the cry of Ofcar's hounds.

C 2

SONG X.

THE BANKS OF HELICON.

De- clare, ye banks of He- li- con, Par naf- sus' hills and

dales ilk one, And foun- tain Cab- al- lein, If o- ny of your

Muf- es all or Nymphis may be per- e- gal Un- to my

la- dy fheen. Or if the la- dies that did lave Their

bo- dies by your brim, So feem- ly were, or yet so swave, So

beau ti- ful or trim. Con- tem- pill, ex- ample take by her
proper port if o- ny so bo- nye a- mang you did re- sort.

No, no. Forſooth was never none,
That with this perfeȼt paragon
    In beauty might compare;
The Muſes would have given the greo
To her as to the A per ſe,
    And peerleſs pearl preclare;
With qualities and form divine,
    By nature ſo decored;
As Goddeſs of all feminine,
    Of men to be adored;
So bleſsed that wiſhed
    She is in all mens thought,
As rareſt and faireſt
    That ever Nature wrought.

It would exceed our limits to give the reſt of the words: the original is in the Pepys Collection in the University of Cambridge. The melody muſt have been a favourite with our anceſtors; for the ſtanza is a very common one in the works of our early poets; many compoſitions, to the tune of The Bánks of Helicon, are to be found in the Bannatyne MS preſerved in the library of the Faculty of Advocates at Edinburgh, compiled in 1568. It is, probably, the moſt ancient Scots tune of which the original words remain.

SIR PATRICK SPENCE.

Very slow.

The King sits in Dun - ferm- line town, drink - ing the blood-red

wine; Oh! where will I get a good sai - lor to sail this ſhip of

mine? Tho' red red glares the wintry sky and winds howl thro' the

bri- ar yet our good ſhip maun face the ſtorm, for Scot- land's faes are near.

2

Then up and fpak an eldren knight ,
  Sat at the King's right knee;
"Sir Patrick Spence is the beft sailor
  "That sails upon the fea."
The King has written a braid letter,
  And fign'd it wi' his hand;
And fent it to Sir Patrick Spence, .
  Was walking on the sand.

3

The firft line that Sir Patrick read,
  A loud laugh laughed he;
The next line that Sir Patrick read,
  The tear blinded his ee.
O wha is this has done this deed,
  This ill deed done to me;
To fend me out this time o' the yeir,
  To fail upon the sea?

4

Mak hafte, mak hafte my merry men all,
  · Our gude fhip fails the morn. —
O fay na sae my mafter dear,
  For I fear a deadlie ftorm.

Late late yeftreen I faw the new moon,
  Wi' the auld moon in her arme;
And I fear, I fear, my mafter dear,
  That we will come to harme.

5

O our Scots nobles were right laith
  To weet their cork-heel'd fhoon;
But lang or a' the play were play'd,
  They wat their heads aboon.
O lang lang may their ladies sit,
  Wi' their fans into their hand,
Or they see gude Sir Patrick Spence
  Cum failing to the land.

6

O lang lang may their ladies ftand
  Wi' their gold kems in their hair,
Waiting to fee their ain dear lords
  For they'll see them nae mair.
Half owre, half owre to Aberdour,
  It's fifty fathom deep;
And there lies gude Sir Patrick Spence,
  Wi' the Scots lords at his feet.

SONG XII.

BRISK WINE.

Dr. Arnold.

Brisk wine brisk wine and lovely women are the

Brisk wine brisk wine and love-ly wo-men are the source the

source of all our joys the source of all our joys; A brimmer

source of all our joys, the source of all our joys; A brimmer

softens ev-'ry care and beauty never never cloys; a brimmer

softens ev-ry care and beauty never never cloys; a brimmer

softens ev-'ry care and beau-ty ne-ver cloys ne-ver

softens ev-ry care, and beauty ne-ver cloys ne-ver

cloys ne-ver cloys and beauty ne-ver cloys and beau-ty

cloys ne-ver cloys and beauty ne-ver cloys and beauty

ne-ver cloys. Then let us drink and let us love while yet our

ner ver cloys. Then let us drink and let us love while yet our

hearts are gay while yet our hearts are gay; Women and wine

hearts are gay while yet our hearts are gay; Women and wine

we all ap-prove as blef-sings night and day as blefsings

we all ap-prove as blef-sings night and day as blessings

night and day. Then let us drink and let us love while yet our

night and day. Then let us drink and let us love while yet our

D

hearts are gay   while yet our hearts are gay - - - - - -   we

hearts are gay - while yet our hearts are gay. Wo- men and wine   we

all - - ap- prove as blef- sings night and day   as blef- sings

all - - ap- prove   as blessings night and day   as blessings

night and day night and   day night and day as blef- sings night and

night and day, night and   day night and day as blef- sings night and

day   as blef- sings night and day.

day   as blef- sings night   and day.

HERE AWA WILLIE.

Here a-wa there a-wa here a-wa Wil-lie! Here a-

wa there a-wa here a-wa hame. Lang have I fought thee

dear have I bought thee, Now I ha'e gotten my Willie a-gain.

Thro' the lang muir I have follow'd my Willie,
Thro' the lang muir I have follow'd him hame;
Whate'er betide us nought fhall divide us,
Love now rewards all my forrow and pain.

Here awa, there awa, here awa, Willie!
Here awa, there awa, here awa hame.
Come, Love, believe me naething can grieve me,
Ilka thing pleafes when Willie's at hame.

D 2

SONG XIV.

PASTHEEN FUEN.

Andantino

A fig for the cares of this whirligig world shall still be

my motto wher- ever I'm twirl'd; From the spring of my youth to the

autumn of life It has chear'd me and whisk'd me thro' trouble and strife.

It has taught me to rise to the summit of ease, By calmly sub-

mitting to for- tune's de- crees. Thus I'm rich with- out pelf for con-

tent is true wealth and the beſt va- de me- cum in ſick-neſs and health.

Juſt as full of defects as the reſt of my kind,
" Give and take" is my meaſure, for *ſpecks* in the mind ;
For who in another ſhould pry for a ſpot,
When he knows in his heart he has blot upon blot ?

In the mere War of Poſts 'twixt the Ins and the Outs,
It but little boots me, who is routed or routs ;
Still I gain by their ſallies, whene'er they combine
To give ſalt to my Muffin, and zeſt to my Wine.

At peace with all ſects, I aſk no man his *Credo*
In points of real import to none I ſay *Cedo*,
Content if my courſe, from the day-break of youth,
Has been ſteer'd by the compaſs and rudder of truth.

Full of life, fun and glee, with a jig in my heel,
Once I revel'd with Bacchus, and joined in the reel ;
But theſe frolics are paſt, and their relics declare,
There's no jig in a crutch, and no reel in a chair.

From a Prodigal, now grown a miſer of Pleaſure,
I begin with Anacreon, to hug my laſt treaſure ;
And the better to manage, and ſpin out my ſtore,
I make one go as far as I uſed to make four.

Light in freight as a Cutter return'd from a cruize,
" Finding little to gain, having little to loſe,*
My anchor is caſt, and my ſails are all furl'd,
" So a fig for the cares of this whirligig world.

* Sancho Panza's conſolatory Proverb—" If little I gain, as little I loſe.''

S O N G XV.

TAKE OH TAKE THOSE LIPS AWAY. *Smith.*

Take, oh take those lips a - way that so sweet - ly

Take, oh take those lips a - way that so sweet- ly

Take, oh take those lips a - way that so sweet - ly

were for- sworn and those eyes the break of day. Lights

were for- sworn and those eyes the dreak of day Lights

were for- sworn, the break of day Lights

that do - - - mis- lead the morn; But my

that do mis- lead the morn;

that do mis- lead the morn; But my

kif - ses bring a - gain, feals of love but feal'd in

But my kiffes bring again, feals of love but feal'd in

kif - ses bring a - gain, feals of love but feal'd in

vain, feals of love but feal'd in vain.

vain, feals of love but feal'd in vain.

vain, feals of love but feal'd in vain.

Take, oh take my fears away,
Which thy cold disdain has bred;
And grant me one aufpicious ray,
From thy morn of beauties fhed:
But thy killing beams reftrain,
Left I be by beauty slain.

SONG XVI.

STIRLING TOWER.

Very slow.

'Twas at the so- lemn mid- night hour Be- fore the first cock's crowing, That weft- lin winds fhook Stirling tow'r, With hol- low mur- murs blowing; When Fan- ny fair all woe- be- gone, Sad on her bed was ly- ing, Lo! thro' the mournful tow'r fhe heard The bo- ding fcreech- owl crying.

O difmal night! fhe faid and wept,
  O night prefaging forrow ;
O difmal night! fhe faid and wept,
  But more I dread to-morrow.

For now the bloody hour draws nigh,
  Each hoft to battle bending ;
At morn fhall fons their fathers flay,
  With deadly hate contending.

Even now in vifions of the night,
  I faw fell death wide fweeping ;
And all the matrons of the land,
  And all the virgins weeping.

And now fhe heard the maffy gates
  Harfh on their hinges turning ;
And now through all the Caftle heard
  The woeful voice of mourning.

Aghaft, fhe ftarted from her bed,
  The fatal tidings dreading ;
O fpeak, fhe cry'd, my father's flain !
  I fee, I fee him bleeding.

"A pale corpse on the fullen fhore,
  At morn, fair maid, I left him ;
Even at the threfh-hold of his gate,
  The foe of life bereft him.

Bold in the battle's front he fell
  With many a wound deformed ;
A braver Knight or better man,
  This fair ifle ne'er adorned."

While thus he fpoke the grief- ftruck maid
  A deadly fwoon invaded ;
Loft was the luftre of her eyes,
  And all her beauty faded.

E

Thefe lines are faid to have been written by the late Sir G. Elliot, on occafion of the death of the celebrated Colonel Gardner, who fell at the battle of Preftonpans, in 1746.

SONG XVII.

MARIA.

Moderato con Espressione.

'Twas

near a thicket's calm re - treat, under a poplar tree, Ma-

ri - a chose her lone- ly seat, to mourn her sorrows free. Her lovely

mourn'd her love not true, and wept her cares a - way.

The brook flow'd gently at her feet
 In murmurs smooth along ;
Her pipe which once she tun'd so sweet
 Had now forgot its song.
No more to charm the vale she tries,
 For grief has fill'd her breast ;
Fled are the joys she used to prize
 And fled with them her rest.

Poor hapless maid, who can behold
 Thy anguish so severe,
Or hear thy love-lorn story told
 Without a pitying tear ?
Maria, hapless maid, adieu !
 Thy sorrows soon must cease;
Soon heav'n will take a maid so true
 To everlasting peace.

THE MARINERS. A GLEE.

We be three poor Ma- ri-ners new- ly come from the Seas; We

We be three poor Ma- ri- ners new- ly come from the Seas; We

We be three poor Ma- ri- ners new- ly come from the Seas; We

fpend our lives in jeo- par- dy while others live at eafe. Shall we go

fpend our lives in jeo- par- dy while o- thers live at eafe. Shall we go

fpend our lives in jeo- par-dy while others live at eafe. Shall we go

dance the round the round the round, fhall we go dance the round the round the

dance the round the round the round, fhall we go dance the round the round the

dance the round the round the round, fhall we go dance the round the round the round; and he that is a jol- ly boy come pledge me on this

round; and he that is a jol- ly boy come pledge me on this

round; and he that is a jol- ly boy come pledge me on this

ground a- ground aground.

ground a- ground a- ground-

ground a- ground a- ground.

We care not for thofe martial men
That do our ftates difdain,
But we care for thofe Merchant men
That do our ftates maintain;
To them we dance this round &c.

SONG XIX.

A CATCH.

Come, come come pull a . way, Boys, Let the glaſ- ses keep

Let their chan - ges be e - qual and their num- ber com-

Thus Mu- sic and Drinking our for- rows ſhall

time to the tune of the Bells that ſo mer- ri- ly ſo mer- ri- ly ſo

pleat; we'll raiſe up the one as the o - ther the o - ther doth

drown; then with joy let us drink off our glaſses, drink off our

mer - ri - ly ding ding ding ding ding ding dong Bell, ding ding ding

ſet, we'll raiſe up the one we'll raiſe up the

glaſses Huz - - za - - - - - Huz- - - za -

ding ding ding dong Bell, fo mer-ri ly chime.

one as the o-ther the o-ther doth fet.

- - Huz-za - - each bumper fhall crown.

SONG XX.

A CATCH.

Strephon the young, the loveliest swain

That e-ver grac'd th'Ar-ca-dian plain,

Fair Ce-lia lov'd nor lov'd in vain.

SONG XXI.

BOW THE HEAD, THOU LILY FAIR.

HAYDN.

Very slow

Bow the head thou li - ly fair, Bow the head in mournful guife,

Sickly turn thy fhining white, Bend thy ftalk and never rife.

Shed thy leaves thou lovely rofe, Shed thy leaves fo fweet and gay; Strow them

wide on the cold earth, Quickly let them fade a - way.

For alas! the gentle knot
  So foftly that did bind
My Emma and her fwain,
  Cruel death has now untwin'd.
Her head with half-clos'd eyes
  Bends upon her breaft of fnow;
Cold and faded are thofe cheeks
  That wont with red to glow.

Mute is that harmonious voice,
  That breath'd the founds of love;
And lifelefs are thofe limbs,
  That with fuch grace did move:
And I of blifs bereft,
  Lone and fad muft ever moan;
Dead to all the world can give,
  Alive to grief alone.

SONG XXII.

CANON.

Byrd.

Non no-bis Do-mi-ne, non no-bis fed no-mi-ni tu-

Non no-bis Do-mi-ne non no-bis fed no-mi-ni

Non no-bis Do-mi-ne non no-bis

o da Glo-ri-am fed nomi-ni tu---o da Glo-ri-

tu-o da Glo-ri-am fed nomini tu-o da

fed nomini tu-o da Glo-ri-am fed nomini

am non no-bis Do-mi-ne non

Glori-am non no-bis Do-mi-

tu-o da Glo-ri-am non

F

LAURA.

Irish Air.

Be - hold the fa - - tal hour ar - rive! Lau - ra

my Lau- ra - ah - fare- well; Se - ver'd from thee

can I sur- vive? From thee whom I have lov'd so

yet - who knows, a - las! who knows If thou wilt

e'er re - mem - ber me!

Along the folitary fhore
  I'll wander, penfive and alone;
And wild re-echoing rocks implore
  To tell me where my nymph is gone.
From early morn to ev'ning's clofe
  My voice fhall ceafelefs call on thee;
And yet who knows, alas! who knows
  If thou wilt e'er remember me!

Oft times I fhall to meads and bow'rs,
  To groves, my former haunts, repair;
Delightful haunts, where once my hours
  Glided in joy, for thou wert there.
There flows the fountain, will I cry,
  Where, blufhing, fcornful fhe would ftand;
Then look with foftly pitying eye,
  And let me feize her yielding hand.

O think what fweet tormenting fmart
  Thy poor forlorn Fileno proves!
O think how faithful is his heart
  Who has no hope, yet hopelefs loves!
Think on the filent fad farewell
  Of him, divided far from thee;
O think! yet who alas! can tell
  If thou wilt e'er remember me.

F 2

O SING UNTO MY ROUNDELAY.

Plaintive.

O sing un-to my round-e-lay O drop the bri-ny

O sing un-to my round-e-lay O drop the bri-ny

tear with me: Dance no more on ho-li-day, Like a run-ning

tear with me: Dance no more on ho-li-day, Like a run-ning

ri-ver be. My love is dead gone to his death-bed All un-der the

ri-ver be. My love is dead, gone to his death-bed All under the

wil-low tree. My love is dead, gone to his death-bed, All

wil-low tree. My love is dead, gone to his death-bed, All

un - der the wil - - low tree.

un- der the wil- low tree.

Black his hair as the winter night,
White his skin as the mountain fnow,
Red his cheek as the morning light,
Cold he lies in the grave below.
My love is dead &c.

SONG XXV.

THE BONNY LASS IN YON TOWN.

Andantino

O wat ye wha's in

yon town, Ye fee the e'en-ing fun u-pon? The dear-eft

Maid's in yon town That e'en-ing fun is fhining on. Now

hap - ly down yon gay green fhaw, She wanders by yon fpreading tree; How bleft ye flow'rs that round her blaw ye catch the glances o' her ee; How

bleft ye birds that near her fing And welcome in the blooming year; And

doubly welcome be the fpring, the feason to my Jeanie dear.

2.

The fun blinks blyth on yon town,
Amang the broomy braes fae green ;
But my delight in yon town,
And deareft pleafure is my Jean :
Without my fair not a' the charms,
O' Paradife could yield me joy ;
But gie me Jeanie in my arms,
And welcome Lapland's dreary fky ;

My cave wad be a lover's bow'r,
Tho' raging winter rent the air ;
And fhe a lovely little flower,
That I wad tent and fhelter there.

Chorus.

O fweet is fhe in yon town,
The finking Sun's gane down upon ;
A fairer than's in yon town,
His fetting beam near fhone upon.

THE COTTAGE MAID.
PLEYEL.

Pastorale, Andante.

Ah! where can

I shed, Hen - ry - is from Lau -

ra fled: Thy love to me thou didst

- im - part, Thy love soon won my

vir - - gin heart; But dear - est Hen - ry thou'st

G

be-   tray'd   thy - - love   with thy poor

Cottage   maid.

Through the vale my grief appears,
Sighing sad with pearly tears;
Oft thy image is my theme,
As I wander on the green;
See from my cheek the colour flies,
And love's sweet hope within me dies;
For O dear Henry thou'st betray'd
Thy love with thy poor Cottage-maid.

JOHN ANDERSON MY JO.

John Anderfon my jo John, ye were my firft conceit, I

think na fhame to fay John, I loe'd ye ear and late ; They

fay you're turning auld John and what tho' it be fo ? ye are

ay the fame kind man to me, John Anderfon my Jo.

John Anderfon my jo John, when we were firft acquaint,
Your lncks were like the raven John, your bonny brow was brent ;
But now ye've turned bald John, your locks are like the fnow,
My bleffings on that frofty pow, John Anderfon my jo.

John Anderfon my jo John, we've feen our bairns bairns,
And yet, my dear John Anderfon, I'm happy in your arms ;
And fae are ye in mine John, I'm fure ye'll no fay no,
Tho' the days are paft, that we have feen, John Anderfon my jo.

John Anderfon my jo John, we've climb'd the hill the gither,
And mony a canty day John, we've had wi' ane anither ;
Now we maun totter down John. but, hand in hand we'll go
And we'll reft the gither at the foot, John Anderfon my jo.

SONG XXVIII.

LIFE HAS NO REAL BLISS.

Slow.

Life has no re - al blifs in ftore; pof - fefs - ing much we

wifh for more, With health with friends with fortune bleft, Why

more for reſt.

II.

But why, whenever Damon's near,
This anxious hope, this pleaſing fear ?
'Tis only friendſhip fills my breaſt ;
And friendſhip ne'er was foe to reſt.

To that his wiſhes ſeem'd to tend,
He only aſkt the name of friend ;
But tho' by looks his flame I gueſt,
Could looks alone have hurt my reſt ?

III.

He ne'er has ſought a ſtudied ſtrain,
In broken words he ſpoke his pain ;
Alas ! ſo much thoſe words expreſt,
I fear 'tis they have ſtol'n my reſt.

But if ſuperior to diſguiſe,
His ſoul is pictur'd in his eyes ;
Of Damon's heart when quite poſſeſt,
I ſoon ſhall find my wonted reſt.

SONG XXIX.

A SHEPHERD ONCE HAD LOST HIS LOVE.

Shepherd once had loft his love; Fal la lal la ral de ral de ra. And as he fought her in the grove;

Fal lal lal la ral de ral de ra. And as he fought her

in the grove, where fhe flept faft as he did ftray, a little bird fung from a spray; Fal lal lal la ral de ral de ra.

In vain this bird did ftrain her throat ;
  Fal,   lal,   lal,   &c.
In vain fhe varied oft her note ;
  Fal,   lal,   lal,   &c.
In vain fhe varied oft her note ;
The foolifh fhepherd wander'd on,
The fair one rofe and foon was gone.
  Fal,   lal,   lal,   &c.

At laft the bird did to him fay,
  Fal,   lal,   lal,   &c.
If you will not when you may,
  Fal,   lal,   lal,   &c.
If you will not when you may,
Oh when you will you fhall have nay :
The little bird then flew away.
  Fal,   lal,   lal,   &c.

SONG XXX.

WE BE SOLDIERS THREE.

We be Soldiers three; Pardonnez moi, Je vous en prie;

We be Soldiers three; Pardonnez moi, Je vous en prie;

We be Soldiers three; Pardonnez moi, Je vous en prie;

lately come forth of the low country, with never a penny of Money.

lately come forth of the low country with never a penny of Money

lately come forth of the low country, with never a penny of Money.

Here good fellow I drink to thee;
 Pardonnez &c.
To all good fellows wherever they be;
 With never &c.

And he that will not pledge me in this,
 Pardonnez &c.
Pays for the shot whatever it is,
 With never &c.

Charge it again Boys charge it again,
 Pardonnez &c.
As long as there is any ink in my pen,
 With never &c.

BRIGHT PHOEBUS.

Bright Phoebus has mounted the chariot of day, And the
horns and the hounds call each sportsman a - way, and the

is in ex - er - cise found. Thro' woods and thro' meadows with

fpeed now they bound, while health ro - sy health is in

ex - er - cife found. Hark a - way! hark a - way!

Hark a - way is the word to the found of the

Horn . . . .

Each hill and each valley is lovely to view,
While Pufs flies the covert and dogs fwift purfue.
Behold where fhe fcours o'er the wide-fpreading plain,
While the loud founding pack purfues her amain.
   Hark away, &c.

At length Pufs is caught and now fighs her laft breath,
And the fhout of the huntfman's the fignal for death;
No joys can delight like the fports of the field;
To hunting all paftimes and pleafures muft yield.
   Hark away, &c.

H 2

SONG XXXII.

YE BIRDS FOR WHOM I REAR'D.

Ye Birds! for whom I rear'd I rear'd the

Ye Birds! for whom I rear'd the

grove, With melt - - - ing lays fa - - - lute my Love! with

grove, With melt - ing lays fa - - lute my Love! with

melt - - ing lays fa - - - lute my Love! My Daphne

melt - ing lays fa - - lute my Love! My Daphne

with your notes de - tain, Or I · have rear'd the grove in

with your notes de - tain, Or I have rear'd the

vain, or   I have   rear'd   the   grove   in   vain.

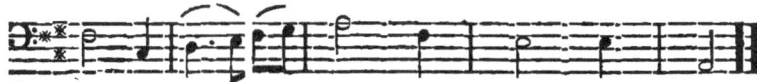

grove, have rear'd the   grove,   the   grove   in   v ain.

Ye flowers! which early fpring fupplies,
Difplay at once your brighteft dyes ;
That fhe your op'ning charms may fee,
Or what were elfe your charms to me.

Ye ftreams! if e'er your banks I lov'd,
If e'er your native founds improv'd ;
May each foft murmur footh my Fair,
Or fure 'twill deepen my defpair.

A SUP OF GOOD WHISKEY.

Allegro.

A sup of good Whiskey will make you glad; Too much of the Creature will make you mad; If you take it in reason 'twill make you wise; If you drink to ex - cefs it will clofe up your eyes; Yet Fa - ther and Mo - ther and Sif - ter and Brother, They all love a

Some Preachers will tell you to drink is bad,
I think fo too——if there's none to be had :
The Swadler will bid you drink none at all, -
But while I can get it, a fig for them all,
  Both Layman and Brother,
  In fpite of this Pother,
Will all take a Sup in their Turn.

Some Doctors will tell ye 'twill hurt your health,
And Juftice will fay, 'twill reduce your wealth,
Phyficians and Lawyers will all agree,
When your money's all gone, they can get no fee ;
  Yet Surgeon and Doctor,
  And Lawyer and Proctor,
Will all take a Sup in their Turn.

The Turks, who arriv'd from the Port fublime,
They told us that drinking was held a great crime ;
Yet after their Dinner, away they flunk,
And tippled their wine, 'till they got quite drunk.
  The Sultan and Crommet,
  And even Mahomet,
They all take a Sup in their Turn.

The Quakers will bid you from drink abftain,
By yea, and by nay, 'tis a fault in the Vain ;
Yet, fome of the Broadbrims will get to the ftuff,
And tipple away 'till they've tippled enough.
  For Stiff rump and Steady,
  And Solomon's Lady,
Would all take a Sup in their Turn.

The Germans will fay they can drink the moft,
The French and Italians will alfo boaft,
Hibernia's the country, for all their noife,
For generous drinking and hearty Boys ;
  There each jovial Fellow,
  Will drink till he's mellow,
And take off his Glafs in his Turn.

SIGH NO MORE LADIES.   *STEVENS.*

Andante.

Sigh no more La - dies, ladies figh no more, men were deceivers

Sigh no more La - dies, ladies figh no more, men were deceivers

ever, men were deceivers ever; one foot on fea and

ever, men were deceivers ever; one foot on fea and

one on fhore, to one thing conftant never, to one thing conftant

one on fhore, to one thing conftant never, to one thing conftant

never. Then figh not fo, but let them go, and be you

never, Then figh not fo, but let them go and be you

blithe and bonny, and be you blithe and bonny, Con-

blithe and bonny, and be you blithe and bonny, Con-

verting all your founds of woe, con - verting all your

verting all your founds of woe, con - verting all your

founds of woe, To hey nony nony hey nony

founds of woe, To hey nony nony; hey nony

nony; hey nony nony; hey nony nony.

nony; hey nony nony; hey nony nony.

Sing no more ditties,
Ladies, fing no more
Of dumps fo dull and heavy;
The frauds of men were ever fo,
Since fummer trees were leafy.

Then figh not fo,
But let them go,
And be you blyth and bonny ;
Converting all your founds of woe
To hey nony nony.

1

IN THE DARK AND LONELY BOWER.

In the dark and lonely bow'r, At the fi - lent

mid - night hour, Let me, let me all a - lone,

Ru - mi - nate on plea - fures gone. Ah! days of blifs de-

light ful days, Could I thofe days of blifs re - ftore, When

fick with love and vain with praife, I figh - ing heard what-

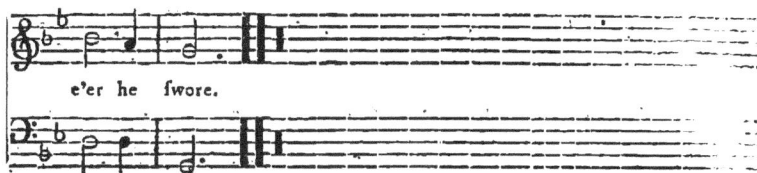

e'er he fwore.

Sadly folemn be the ftrain;
Suited to a heart in pain;
Mirth and pleafure I forego,
Welcome forrow, welcome woe :
Too long in folly's court I ftray'd,
A fond and witlefs maid I ween ;
Ah faithlefs fwain ! how oft he faid,
No nymph fo fair he e'er had feen.

Beauty fades, and youth retires,
And mirth's airy train expires,
Wiping tears from pity's eye,
Waiting loves are hovering nigh :
Let virgin-hands frefh flow'rs fupply,
To ftrew a haplefs virgin's bier ;
Ah perjur'd fwain ! Can you deny
To drop a fad relenting tear !

I 2

SONG XXXVI.

TIBBIE FOWLER.

Slow.

Tibbie Fowler o' the glen there's o'er mony woo-in at her, Tibbie Fowler o' the glen, there's o'er mo-ny wooin at her. Wooin at her, pu-in at her, courtin her, and can-na get her: Filthy elf, its for her pelf, that a' the lads are wooin at her.

Ten cam' eaſt and ten came weſt,
Ten came rowin o'er the water;
Twa came down the lang dyke ſide,
There's twa and thirty wooin at her.
   Wooin at her &c.

There's ſeven but, and ſeven ben,
Seven in the pantry wi' her;
Twenty head about the door,
There's ane. and forty wooin at her.
   Wooin at her &c.

She's got pendles in her lugs,
Cockle ſhells wad ſet her better;
High heel'd ſhoon and filler tags,
And a' the lads are wooin at her.
   Wooin at her &c.

Be a laſſie e'er ſae black,
An ſhe hae the name o' filler;
Set her upo' Tintock-tap,
The wind will blaw a man till her.
   Wooin at her &c.

Be a laſſie e'er ſae fair,
An ſhe want the penny filler;
A flie may fell her in the air,
Before a man be even'd till her,
   Wooin at her &c.

O I HAE SEEN THE ROSES BLAW. *Mr. Muschet.*

O! I hae feen the roses blaw, The heather bloom, the

broom an a', The li-ly fpring as white as fnaw, Wi' a' their native

fplendor: Yet Mary's fweeter on the green, as frefh an' fair as

Flora queen, Mair ftately than the branching bean, and like the i-vy

slender. In nature like a fummer day, transcendent as a

funny ray, Her shape and air is frank an' gay, wi' a' that's

sweet an' tender.

II.

While lavrocks sing their chearfu' lays,
An' shepherds brush the dewy braes,
To meet wi' Mary's bonny face,
    Amang the shades I wander.
My captive breast, (by fancy led)
Adores the sweet the lovely maid,
We ilka smile and charm array'd,
    To make a heart surrender.
I love her mair than bees do flow'rs,
Or birks the spreading leafy bow'rs;
Her presence yields me what the show'rs,
    To hills and valleys render.

III.

Cou'd I obtain my charmer's love,
Mair stable than a rock I'd prove;
Wi' a' the meekness of a dove,
    To ilka pleasure hand her:
If she wad like a shepherd lad,
I'd change my cane for crook an' plaid,
Upon the hill tune up the reed,
    An' wi' a sang commend her.
For her I'd live a life remote,
Wi' her I'd love a rustic cott,
There bless kind fortune for my lot,
    And ilka comfort lend her.

SONG XXXVIII.

THE SAILOR BOY.

Poll dang it how d'ye do? Nan, won't you

g'us a buſs? Why, what's to do with you? Why here's a pretty

fuſs! Why what's to do wi' you; why here's a pretty

fuſs; Say, ſhan't we kiſs and toy? I goes to ſea no more;

Oh! I'm the Sai-lor Boy for ca-per-ing a- shore,

Oh! I'm the Sailor Boy for ca-per-ing a- shore.

II.
Father he apprentic'd me
All to a Coafting Ship,
I b'ing refov'd d'ye fee,
To give 'em all the flip,
I got to Yarmouth Fair,
Where I had been before,
So Father found me there,
A Capering a fhore.

III.
Next out to India,
I went a Guinea Pig,
We got to table Bay,
But mind a pretty rig,
The Ship driving out to Sea,
Left me and many more,
Among the Hottenpots
A Capering a fhore.

IV.
I loves a bit of Hop,
Life's ne'er the worfer for't,
If in my wake fhou'd drop,
A Fiddle, " that's your fort;"
Thrice tumble up a hoy
Once get the labour o'er,
Then fee the Sailor Boy,
A Capering a fhore.

K

IN THE DEAD OF THE NIGHT.

In the
dead of the night, when with labour op - - preſt, All
mortals enjoy the calm bleſſings of eaſe, Cupid knock'd at my window diſ-
turbing my reſt, Who's there I de- mand- ed, Who's

there I de - mand - ed, Be - - gone if you pleafe.

II.

He anfwer'd fo meekly, fo modeft and mild,
Dear Ma'am it is I, an unfortunate child;
'Tis a cold rainy night, I am wet to the fkin,
And I have loft my way Ma'am, fo pray let me in.

III.

No fooner from cold and from wet he got eafe,
Than taking his bow, he faid, Ma'am if you pleafe,
If you pleafe, Ma'am faid he, from experience I'd know,
If the rain has not damaged the ftring of my bow.

IV.

Away trip'd the urchin, as brifk as a bee,
And laughing, I wifh you much joy Ma'am, faid he,
My bow is not damaged, nor yet is my dart,
But you will have trouble in bearing the fmart.

K 2

SONG XL.

THE GARRETEER.

Happy the man who life's dull cares to low am-bi-tion gives; And mounting up five pair of stairs, In lof-ty gar-ret lives. While tu-mults vex our earth-ly ball, Our streets while noi-sy cries, The Garret-teer ef-capes them all, The Gar-ret-teer ef-capes them all "com-mer-cing with the skies."

No wrangling mobs, thus heard from far,
   Difturb his tranquil foul :
The rattling coach, and rumbling car,
   Like diftant thunders roll.

Proud as a fultan on his throne,
   His vaffals at his feet :
Above the world, the bard looks down,
   On all that man thinks great.

Whilft duft or fmoke beneath him rolls,
   He fnuffs th' ætherial breeze ;
And broils his fteak upon the coals,
   Or calmly toafts his cheefe.

The fpider in the bard's bleft dome,
   His web with fafety hides ;
Where mops or brooms dare never come,
   " That come to all" befides.

The wheezing dun, one flight of ftairs,
   Who mounts to feize his prey,
To ftorm his citadel defpairs,
   And growling turns away.

The Cambrian thus on Penmanmoor,
   Or Snowdon's lofty fide,
Amidft his craggy rocks fecure,
   The Roman power defy'd.

SONG XLI.

PAUVRE MADELON.

Could

you to battle march a - way, And leave me here com

plain - ing? Could you to battle march a - way, And leave me here com - plain - ing? I'm sure 'twould break my heart to stay when

you were gone cam - paign - ing; Ah! non non non, Pauvre Made-

lon will ne - ver quit her Ro - ver Ah!

non non non, Pauvre Ma - de - lon wou'd go with you

all the world o - ver.

CONTINUED:

II.

Soldier.—Cheer cheer, my love, you shall not grieve,
    A Soldier true you'll find me ;
I cou'd not have the heart to leave
    My little girl behind me.
Ah non, non, non, Pauvre Madelon
    Shall never quit her Rover ;
Ah non, non, non, Pauvre Madelon
    Shall go with me all the world over.

III.

Madelon.—And can you to the battle go
    To womens' fears a stranger ?
No fears my breast will ever know
    But when my love's in danger.
Ah, non, non, non, Pauvre Madelon
    Will never quit her Rover ;
Ah, non, non, non, Pauvre Madelon
    Will go with you all the world over.

Duet.—Then let the world jog as it will,
    Let hollow friends forsake us ;
We both shall be as happy still,
    As love and war can make us.
Ah, non, non, &c.

OTHER WORDS TO THE SAME AIR.

From night till morn, I take my glass,
    In hopes to forget my Chloe ;
But as I take the pleasing draught,
    She's ne'er the less before me.
Ah, no, no, no, wine cannot cure
    The pain I endure for my Chloe.

To wine I flew to ease the smart
    Her beauteous charms created ;
But wine more firmly bound the chain,
    And love would not be cheated.
Ah, no, no, &c.

SONG XLII.

TELL ME THOU DEAR DEPARTED SHADE.

Tell me thou dear de - part - ed Shade, Ah tell me

Tell me thou dear de - part - ed Shade, Ah tell me

whither art thou flown; To what de - lightful place

whither art thou flown; To what de - lightful place

con - vey'd, What dif - tant World to me un - known;

con - vey'd, What dif - tant world to me unknown,

What world - - - - - - what dif - tant

What dif - tant world to me uu - known, what dif - tant

world to me un - known. Say

world to me un - known. Say

L

does thy ai - ry flight ex - tend, As far as

does thy ai - ry flight ex - tend As far as

our once fav' - rite bow'r, Doft thou my lone- ly

our once fav - rite bow'r, Doft thou my lonely

walks at - tend, or visit me at mid - night

walks at - tend, or visit me at mid - night

hour, or visit me at mid - night hour?

hour, or visit me at mid - night hour?

Larghetto

When Sol difplays his radiant beam, each thought I de- di-

When Sol difplays his radiant beam, each thought I de - di-

cate to thee, each thought I de - di - cate to thee. And

cate to thee, each thought I de - di - cate to thee. And

if thou form'ft the night - ly dream, the night - - -

if thou form'ft the night- ly dream, How foothing then is

. . ly dream, How foothing then is sleep to me! And

sleep to me! How foothing then is sleep to me! And

if thou form'ft the night - ly dream, How footh - ing then is

if thou form'ft the night- ly dream, How footh - ing then is

sleep to me, How foothing then is sleep to me!

sleep to me, How foothing then is sleep to me!

SONG XLIII.

BONNY DOWN.

Ye banks and braes of Bon - ny Down, How can you bloom so

fresh and fair; How can ye sing ye lit - tle birds, While

I'm sae wae and full of care. Thou'lt break my heart

lit - tle birds, That want - on through the flowering thorn, You

mind me of de - - - par - ted joys, De - part - ed ne - ver

to re - turn.

II,

Oft have I roam'd by bonny Down,
To fee the rofe and woodbine twine,
Where ilka bird, fung o'er its note,
And chearfully I join'd with mine.
Wi' heartfom glee I pull'd a rofe,
A rofe out of yon thorny tree:
But my falfe love has ftol'n the rofe,
And left the thorn behind to me.

SONG XLIV.

SALLY IN OUR ALLEY.

Of all the girls that are so smart, There's none like pret-ty Sally - -; She is the dar-ling of my heart, And she lives in our - - Al-ley; There's ne'er a La - dy in the land, That's half so sweet as Sally - ; She is the dar-ling of my heart, And she lives in our Al-ley.

II.

Her father he makes cabbage nets,
　And thro' the streets does cry 'em;
Her mother she sells laces long,
　To such as please to buy 'em:
But by such folks was never bred,
　So sweet a girl as Sally,
She is the darling of my heart,
　And she lives in our Alley.

III.

Of all the days that's in the week,
　I dearly love but one day;
And that's the day, that comes betwixt,
　The Saturday and Monday:
For then I'm drest in all my best,
　To walk abroad with Sally;
　　She is &c-

IV.

My master he takes me to church,
　And often am I blamed;
Because I leave him in the lurch,
　As soon as text is named;
I leave the church in sermon time,
　And slink away to Sally;
　　She is &c,

V.

When Christmas comes about again,
　Oh! then I shall have money;
I'll hoard it up, and box and all,
　I'll give it to my honey;
And wou'd it were ten thousand pounds!
　I'd give it all to Sally;
　　She is &c,

SONG XLV.

FICKLE STREPHON.

To dear A - ma - ryllis young Strephon had long declar'd his fix't

paſſion, and dy'd for in ſong, He went one May morning to

meet in the grove, By her own dear appointment, this goddeſs of love.

Mean time in his mind all her charms he ran

o'er And doated on each, and doated on each

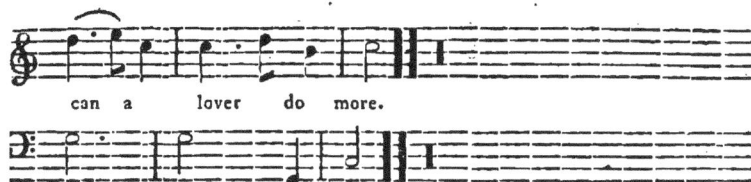

can   a   lover   do   more.

He waited and waited ; then changing his ftrain
'Twas fury, and rage, and defpair, and difdain !
The fun was commanded to hide his dull light,
And the whole courfe of nature was alter'd downright,
'Twas his haplefs fortune to die and adore,
But never to change—can a lover do more ?

Cleora, it happ'd came by accident there,
No rofe-bud fo tempting, no lily fo fair ;
He prefs'd her white hand-next her lips he effay'd,
Nor would fhe deny him, fo civil the maid !
Her kindly compliance his peace did reftore;
And dear Amaryllis—was thought of no more.

`M

SONG XLVI.

NIGHT TO LOVERS JOYS A FRIEND.

Night, to lovers joys a friend, Swiftly thy af-sist-ance yield; Lock up envious fee-ing day, Bring the wil-ling youth a-way.

Hafte and fpeed the tedious hour, To the secret happy

bow'r, Then, my heart, for blifs pre - pare, Thyrfis fure - ly

will be there; Thyrsis furely will be there.

See the hateful day is gone,
Welcome ev'ning now comes on;
Soon to meet my dear I fly,
None but Love fhall then be by;
None fhall dare to venture near,
To tell the plighted vows they hear;
Parting thence will be the pain,
But we'll part to meet again.

Farewell loitring idle day!
To my fwain I hie away,
On the wings of Love I go,
He the ready way will fhew.
Peace, my breaft, nor danger fear,
Love and Thyrsis both are near;
'Tis the youth! I'm fure 'tis he!
Night, how much I owe to thee!

M 2

Stay travel-ler; tarry here to night; The rain yet beats, the wind is loud, The moon has too with-drawn her light And gone to sleep behind a cloud; 'Tis

·S.

foul to tell the rea - dy way. Come deareſt Kate our &c.

Come deareſt Kate, our meal prepare, | Approach the hearth, there take a place,
This ſtranger ſhall partake our beſt ; | And till the hour of reſt draws nigh,
A cake and raſher be his fare, | Of Robin-Hood and Chevy-Chace
With ale that makes the weary bleſt. | We'll ſing ; then to our pallets hie ;

Had I the means I'd uſe you well, 'Tis lit - tle I have

got to boaſt ; Yet ſhou'd you of this cot - tage tell, Say

Hal the Woodman was your hoſt ; Say Hal the Woodman

was your · hoſt.

SONG XLVIII.

SOMEBODY.

Pastorale.

Were I ob-lig'd to beg my bread and

had not where to lay my head; I'd creep where yon - der herds are

fed, And steal a look at Some-bo - dy; My own dear

Somebo- dy, my con - ftant Some-bo- dy; I'd creep where yonder

herds are fed, And fteal a look at Some - bo - dy.

Ah! fhould my chafte love meet return,
I'd blefs the day that I was born;
And never more would figh forlorn,
But live to look at Somebody.
With him I'd tend my fleecy care,
With him each anxious .wifh I'd fhare,
And only ask that I might bear
The name of my dear Somebody.

SONG XLIX.

THOU DEAR SEDUCER.

FISHER.

Thou dear fe - du - cer of my heart, Fond caufe of ev - 'ry

ftruggling figh, No more can I   con - ceal love's fmart, No more re-ftrain the

ar - dent eye. What tho' this tongue did ne - ver move, To tell thee all . its

mafter's pain ;   My   eyes, my looks, have fpoke my love ; Al -

vi - na fhall they fpeak in vain fhall they fpeak in vain. - - - What

tho' this tongue did ne - - ver fpeak to tell thee all its

Mafter's pain my eyes my looks have fpoke my love, Al -

Adagio.

vi - na fhall they fpeak in vain, fhall they fpeak,

Andantino.

fhall they fpeak fhall they fpeak in vain?

N

II.

For ſtill imagination warm,
    Preſents thee at the noontide beam ;
And ſleep gives back thy angel form,
    To claſp thee in the midnight dream,
Alvina, tho' no ſplendid ſtore
    Of riches more than merit move ;
Yet charmer, I am far from poor,
    For I am more than rich in love.

III.

Pulſe of my beating heart, ſhall all
    My gay ſeducive hopes be fled,
Unheeded wilt thou hear me fall,
    Unpitied wilt thou ſee me dead ?
I'll make a cradle of this breaſt,
    Thy image all its Child ſhall be ;
My throbbing heart ſhall rock to reſt,
    The cares that waſte my life and me.

IN VAIN I TRY MY EVERY ART.

Slow.

In vain I try my ev - ry art, Nor can I

fix a single heart, Yet I'm not old nor ug - ly.

Let me con - fult my faith - ful glafs, A face much

worfe than this might pafs, Me - thinks I look full fmug - ly.

Yet blefs'd with all thefe powerful charms,
The young Philemon fled my arms,
  That wild unthinking rover ;
Hope, filly maids, as foon to bind
The rolling ftream, the flying wind,
  As fix a rambling lover.
But hamper'd in the marriage noofe,
In vain they ftruggle to get loofe.
  And make a mighty riot :
Like madmen how they rave and ftare !
A while they fhake their chains and fwear,
  And then lie down in quiet.

SONG LI.

SIR EGLAMORE.

SHIELD.

Sir Eg-la-more was a valiant knight, Fa la lan-ky down dilly, He call'd for his sword and went forth to fight, Fa la lanky down dilly, He went forth to fight as I've heard the folk say, And when he came there he ran away.

CONTINUED:

Fa la la la la la   lanky down   dilly,   Fa la la la la la

lanky down   dilly.

II.

A hungry wolf did tow'rd him leap,
    Fa la lanky down dilly,
But he'd rather met with a fcore of fheep,
    Fa la lanky down dilly :
Then he ran fo faft that his fword did drop,
And he fcorn'd to turn back to pick it up,
    Fa la &c.

III.

Then there came whiftling down the plain,
    Fa la &c.
A furly fturdy dauntlefs fwain,
    Fa la &c.
Mean while the knight ran up a tree,
That if they fhould fight he the combat might fee,
    Fa la &c.

IV.

Oh then began a bloody fray,
    Fa la &c,
As the knight durft not fight, he refolv'd to pray,
    Fa la &c.
But had you beheld Sir Eglamore,
When as he heard the favage roar,
    Fa la &c.

V.

The peafant did his ribs fo roaft,
    Fa la &c,
That mafter wolf gave up the ghoft,
    Fa la &c.
So when Sir Knight faw the monfter dead,
His courage return'd and he cut off his head,
    Fa la &c.

SONG LII.

FAIR FIDELE.

ARNE.

To fair Fi - - de - le's graſ - - ſy tomb, Soft maids and

village hinds ſhall bring each op' - ning ſweet of

ear-lieft bloom, and ri - fle all the breath - - ing

fpring.

II.

No wailing ghoft fhall dare appear
   To vex with fhrieks this quiet grove ;
But fhepherd lads affemble here,
   And melting virgins own their love.

III.

No wither'd witch fhall here be feen ;
   No goblins lead their nightly crew,
The female fays fhall haunt the green ;
   And drefs thy grave with early dew.

IV.

The redbreaft oft at ev'ning hours
   Shall kindly lend his little aid,
With hoary mofs and gather'd flowr's
   To deck the ground where thou art laid.

V.

When howling winds and beating rain
   In tempeft fhake the fylvan cell,
Or midft the chace upon the plain
   The tender thought on thee fhall dwell.

VI.

Each lonely fcene fhall thee reftore ;
   For thee the tear be duly fhed,
Belov'd till life can charm no more,
   And mourn'd till pity's felf be dead.

S O N G LIII.

GIN A BODY MEET A BODY.

Gin a bo-dy meet a bo-dy, Coming thro' the rye:

Gin a bo-dy kiſs a bo-dy Need a bo-dy cry?

Il-ka bo-dy has a bo-dy ne'er a ane ha'e I, But

a' the lads they loe me weel, And what the deuce care I?

Gin a body meet a body coming thro' the broom,
Gin a body kiſs a body need a body gloom?
Ilka Jenny has her Jocky, ne'er a ane ha'e I,
But a' the lads they loe me weel, and what the deuce care I?

SONG LIV.

A CATCH; For three voices.

Hail, flow'-ry meads foft pur-ling rill - and

Where oft I've ftray'd with Stre-phon dear - - eft

Witnefs ye facred haunts each herb and

grove; ye fweet re-treats of in-no-cence and love;

youth whofe voice was mu-fic and whofe foul was truth;

flow'r, how much his cru-el fate I now de-plore.

O.

SONG LV.

COME LIVE WITH ME.

Andante.   *WEBBE.*

Come live with me, come come live with me and be my love,

Come live with me, come, come live with me and be my

And we will all the pleasures prove we will all the pleasures

love; And we will all the plea - sures

prove that grove and valley hill and field or woods and ftee - py

prove that grove and valley hill and field or woods and ftee - py

mountains yield; And I will make thee beds of rofes, And twine

mountains yield; And I will make thee beds of rofes And twine and

- - a thoufand fragrant pofies; A cap of flow'rs and ru - ral

twine a thoufand fragrant pofies; A cap of flow'rs and rural kirtle, Em - broider'd all with leaves of myrtle.

kirtle, Em - broider'd all with leaves of myrtle.

Paſtorale.

A belt of ſtraw and i - vy buds, A co - ral

A belt of ſtraw and i - vy buds, A co - ral

clasp and am - ber ſtuds; And if theſe pleaſures

claſp and amber ſtuds; And if theſe pleaſures

may - thee move, Then come with me - and be my

may thee move, Then come with me and be my

love. The ſhepherd ſwains' ſhall dance - and ſing For

love. The Shepherd ſwains ſball dance and ſing For

O 2

thy de - light each May mor - ning. If joys like thefe thy

thy de - light each May mor - ning. If joys - like thefe thy

mind - may move, Then live with me and be my love; If

mind may move, Then live with me and be my love; If -

joys like thefe thy mind - may move, Then live with

joys like thefe thy mind may move, Then live with

me and be my love.

me and be my love.

SONG LVI.

THE ANSWER TO "COME LIVE WITH ME."

Andante.

If love and all the world were young, And truth in ev - ry

If love and all the world were young, and truth in ev - ry

fhepherd's tongue, Thy fancied pleafures might me move, And

fhepherd's tongue, Thy fancied pleafures might me move, And

I might liften to thy love, I might liften

I might lift - en to thy love, I might liften

to thy love. But time drives flocks drives flocks, from field to fold;

to thy love. But time drives flocks from field to fold, Then

Then ri - - vers rage, then ri - vers rage then ri - vers rage.

ri - vers rage - rage and

and hills grow cold, grow cold, grow cold Then drooping Philo-

hills grow cold - - - grow cold, Then drooping Philo-

mel is dumb, And age complains of care to come, Then drooping Philo-

mel is dumb, And age complains of care to come, Then drooping Philo-

mel is dumb, And age complains of care to come.

mel is dumb, And age complains of care to come.

Pastorale.

Thy gowns thy belts thy beds of roses, Thy

Thy belts thy beds of roses, Thy

cap thy kir-tle and thy po-fies, All

cap thy kir-tle and thy po-fies, All

thefe in me in me can no-thing move To

thefe in me can no - thing move To

live with thee and be thy love. If youth could

live with thee and be thy love. If youth could

laft and love ſtill breed? Had joys no date and

laft and love ftill breed; Had joys no date and

age no need; Then thefe de-lights my mind might

age no need: Then thefe de-lights my mind might

move, And I might liſt-en to thy love.

move, And I might lift - en to thy love.

SONG LVII.

THE POOR LITTLE GIPSEY.

A poor little Gypſey I wander for - lorn; my fortune was told long be- fore I was born, ſo fortunes I tell as for - - ſaken I stray and in search of my love I am lost on my way;

Spare a half-penny, spare a half-penny spare a

poor little Gipsey, a Gipsey a halfpenny, Spare a

poor little Gypsey a halfpenny.

I fear from this line you have been a sad man,
And to harm us poor girls have form'd many a plan ;
Beware lest repentance too late cause you pain,
And attend to the lesson I give in my strain.
     Spare a &c.

Thro' wilds and thro' forests as wearied I roam,
Long absent from friends, from parents and home,
Tho' sad is my heart and tho' sore are my feet,
Yet I sing on my way thus to all that I meet,
     Spare a &c.

P

SONG LVIII.

COMING THRO' THE CRAIGS O' KYLE.

Coming thro' the craigs o' Kyle, A - mang the bonny blooming heather, There I met a bonny laſſie, Keeping a' her ewes to - gether. O'er the moor a - mang the heather, O'er the moor a - mang the heather, There I met a bo - nie laſſie keeping a' her ewes to - gether.

II.

Says I, my dear, where is thy hame,
In moor or dale, pray tell me whether,
She says I tent the fleecy flocks
That feed amang the blooming heather.
  O'er the moor &c.
  O'er the moor &c.
She fays I tent the fleecy flocks
That feed amang the blooming heather.

III.

We fat us down upon a bank,
Sae warm and funny was the weather,
She left her flocks at large to rove
Amang the bonny blooming heather.
  O'er the moor &c.
  O'er the moor &c.
She left her flocks at large to rove,
Amang the bonny blooming heather.

IV.

She charm'd my heart and ay finfyne
I can na think on any ither,
By fea and fky fhe fhall be mine,
The bonny lafs amang the heather.
  O'er the moor &c.
  O'er the moor &c.
By fea and fky fhe fhall be mine,
The bonny lafs amang the heather.

SONG LIX.

SHE CAME FROM THE HILLS.

She came from the hills of the West, A smile of con - tentment she

wore; Her heart was a garden of reft, But ah! the fweet

fea - son is o'er. How oft by the ftreams in the

wood, De - lighted fhe'd ramble and rove; And while fhe ftood marking the flood, Would tune up a stan - za of

love.

II.

Her drefs was a garment of green,
 Set off with a border of white;
And all the day long might be feen
 Like a bird that is always in plight.
In rural diverfion and play
 The Summers glid fmoothly along;
And her winters pafs'd brifkly away,
 Cheer'd up with a tale or a fong.

III.

At length a deftroyer came by,
 A youth of more perfon than parts,
Well fkill'd in the arts of the eye,
 The conqueft and havock of hearts.
He led her by fountains and ftreams,
 He woo'd her with fonnets and books;
He told her his tales and his dreams,
 And mark'd their effect in her looks.

IV.

He taught her by midnight to roam
 Where fpirits and fpectres affright;
For paffions increafe with the gloom,
 And caution expires with the light.
At length, like a Rofe from the fpray,
 Like a lily juft pluckt from the ftem,
She droopt, and fhe faded away,
 Thrown by and neglected like them.

SONG LX.

YESTERDAY.

Slow.

Say ye studious grave and old, Tell me all ye

fair and gay, Tell me where I may be-hold The

fleet - ing forms of Yest - er - day. Where's Au - tumnal

plen - ty sped, Winter where's thy boistrous sway; Where's the vernal flow' - ret fled, Summer where's thy Yefter -

day, Summer where's thy Yef - terday.

Jocund fprites' of focial joy,
Round our fmiling goblet play;
Flit ye pow'rs of rude annoy,
Like the ghoft of Yefterday.

Brim the bowl, and pafs it round
Lightly tune the fportive lay ;
Let the feftal hour be crown'd
E.'er 'tis loft like Yefterday.

HOW LONG AND DREARY IS THE NIGHT.

How long and dreary is the night, When I am frae my Dearie; I sleeplefs lye frae e'en to morn Tho' I were ne'er fo weary: I sleeplefs lye frae e'en to morn tho' I were ne'er fo weary.

When I think on the happy days,
I fpent wi' you my Dearie;
And now what lands between us lie,
How can I be but eerie!
    And now what lands &c.

How flow ye move ye heavy hours,
As ye were wae and weary,
It was na fae ye glented by,
When I was wi' my Dearie.
    It was na fae ye glented, &c.

SONG LXII.

A CATCH FOR THREE VOICES.

Hail, hail, green fields and fha - dy woods hail cryftal

Hail, Nature's un - corrupted goods where virtue

Free from vice, - - - - - and free -

ftreams that ftill run pure; Hail cryft- - al ftreams

oo - ly dwells fe - cure, where vir - tue

- - from care; Age has no pain nor youth a -

that ftill that ftill run - pure.

on - ly dwells fe - cure,

fnare nor youth a fnare.

SONG LXIII.

AH TELL ME WHY SHOULD SILLY MAN.

Ah! tell me why should sil - ly man, Thus mif - ap - ply his fhort fo - journ, Thus wafte the life that's but a fpan, The mi - nutes that fhall ne'er re - turn? If he with thankful lip would tafte, The pleafures

caſt, But ſun-ſhine deck his hap-py day; But ſun-ſhine

deck his hap-py day.

'Tis not the biting wintry blaſt,
'Tis not the ſcorching ſummer ſky,
'Tis not the coaſt on which he's caſt,
Or where he's born or where ſhall die:

No — independent quite of theſe,
The joys or anguiſh he muſt find ;
No ſun can ſcorch, no froſt can freeze
The joys of a contented mind.

Q 2

SONG LXIV.

THE PRIMROSE GIRL.

Come,   buy of poor Kate, Primroses I fell; Thro' London's fair

ci - ty I'm known very well. Tho' my heart is quite funk, yet I   constantly cry, Come, who'll buy Prim - rofes, who'll buy Prim - rofes,

who'll buy Primro - fes, who'll buy, who'll buy?

My friends are all dead, I'm look'd on with fcorn;
Ah! better for me I had never been born:
Tho' I'm poor I am honeft, and oft heave the figh,
While crying Primrofes, who'll buy Primrofes, &c.

To virtue when thus with forrow allied,
The tear of compafsion will not be denied;
Then pity poor Kate who plaintively cries,
Come, who'll buy Primrofes, who'll buy Primrofes, &c.

SAVOURNA DELISH.

Oh! the moment was sad when my love and I parted, Sa - vourna De - lish Shighan Oh! As I kifs'd off her tears, I was nigh broken bearted, Sa - vourna De - lish Shighan Oh.

Wan was her cheek which

hung on my fhoulder, damp was her hand no marble was colder, I

felt that I ne-ver a-gain fhould behold her; Sa - vourna De-lifh

Shighan Oh.

II.

When the word of command put our men into motion,
> Savourna &c.
I buckled my knapfack to crofs the wide ocean,
> Savourna &c.
Brifk were our troops all roaring like thunder,
Pleaf'd with the voyage, impatient for plunder,
My bofom with grief was almoft torn afunder.
> Savourna &c.

III.

Long I fought for my country far far from my true love,
> Savourna &c,
All my pay and my booty I hoarded for you love,
> Savourna &c.
Peace was proclaim'd, efcap'd from the flaughter,
Landed at home, my fweet girl, I fought her,
But forrow alas! to her cold grave had brought her,
> Savourna &c.

SONG LXVI.

WHEN YOUTH'S SPRIGHTLY FLOOD.

When youth's fprightly flood roll'd high in my blood, this heart never ·funk at a foe; this heart never funk, never funk never funk this heart never funk at a foe; never never never funk at a foe ; With true Britiſh pride. I've

oftentimes try'd, the faulchion inſtead of the plow ; With

true Britiſh pride, I've oftentimes try'd the faulchion inſtead of the

plow ; the faulchion inſtead of the plow.

Then Britain was

R

glorious, and always victorious, then Britain was glorious and

always victorious.

ARNE.

And Briton ftill bears,
Swains fit for her wars,
Whofe hearts glow with liberty's fire;
My girls throw away,
Your fears for a day,
For beauty can valour infpire ;
Till Britain is glorious,
And once more victorious.

SONG LXVII.

ARIEL'S SONG IN THE TEMPEST.

ARNE.

Where the bee ſucks there lurk I; In a cow - slips bed I lye, There I couch when owls do cry, when owls do cry, when owls do cry; On the bat's back do I fly - - - -

Af - ter fun-fet mer-ri-ly, mer-ri-ly, af - ter funfet mer - ri -

ly.

Mer - ri-ly, mer - ri-ly, fhall I live now, Under the

bloffom that hangs on the bough; Merrily, merrily, fhall I live now, Under the bloſſom that hangs on the bough, Under the

bloſſom that hangs on the bough.

SONG LXVIII.

WHAT BLEST HOURS.

LINLEY.

What bleft hours un - tainted with for - row does the

maiden prove who knows not love, so merrily so merri - ly

merrily fo merri - ly fhe sings thro' the day:

Dull forrow fhall threaten in

vain, the de - light of her heart to re - ftrain; While from Cupid

free, bleft in li - berty not a figh fhe blends with the ftrain;

While from Cu - pid free bleft in li - ber - ty not a figh fhe

blends with the ftrain. What bleft hours un - tainted by forrow, does the maiden prove who knows not love, fo merrily fo

merri - ly merrily fo merri - ly fhe mer - ri- ly fings thro' the

day. As fhe

gay - ly carols a - long, Let me join let me join

fweet freedom's fong, Oh may my heart ever bear a part in the

hap - py maid ſo blithe - ly ſo blithe - ly ſings thro' the

day .

SINCE I'M BORN A MORTAL MAN.

Larghetto.

Since I'm born a mor - tal man, And my be - ing's

Since I'm born a mor - tal man, And my be - ing's

Moderato.

but a span, 'Tis a march that I muft make, 'Tis a journey

but a span, 'Tis a march that I muft make, 'Tis a journey

I muft take : What is paft I know full well, what is future

I muft take : What is paft I know full well, what is future

who can tell ? What is paft I know full well, what is future

who can tell ? What is paft I know full well, what is future

Allegro.

who can tell ? Tea - zing care then fet me free

who can tell ? Tea - zing care then fet me free

What have I to do with thee? Tea - zing care what have

what have I to do with thee? what have

I to do with thee? What have I to do with thee?

I to do with thee? Teazing care what have I to do with thee?

All my fhort liv'd hours fhall fhine, Thus re - plete with mirth and wine

All my fhort liv'd hours fhall fhine, Thus re - plete with mirth and wine,

All my fhort liv'd hours fhall fhine, Thus replete with mirth and wine

All my fhort liv'd hours fhall fhine, Thus replete with mirth and wine

All my fhort liv'd hours fhall fhine, Thus re - plete with mirth and wine

All my fhort liv'd hours fhall fhine; Thus re - plete with mirth and wine

CONTINUED.

Thus re - plete with mirth and wine ; Thus re - plete with

Thus re - plete with mirth and wine ; Thus replete with

mirth and wine.

mirth and wine.

SONG LXX.

LET US ALL BE UNHAPPY TOGETHER.

We bipeds made up of frail clay, A - las are the children of

forrow ; And tho' brifk and merry to day, We all may be wretched to-

morrow ; For funfhine's fucceeded by rain, Then fearful of life's ftormy

weather, Left pleafure fhould only bring pain ; Let us

all be un-happy to - - gether, Let us all be un-happy together, Let us all be un - happy to - - gether, For

funshine's succeeded by rain; Then, fearful of life's stormy

weather, Left pleasure should on - ly bring pain, Let us

all be un - happy to - - gether.

II.

I grant, the best blessing we know
Is a friend,—for true friendship's a treasure,
And yet, lest your friend prove a foe,
Oh taste not the dangerous pleasure,

Thus friendſhip's a ſlimſy affair,
   Thus riches and health are a bubble ;
Thus there's nothing delightful but care,
   Nor any thing pleaſing but trouble.

III.

If a mortal would point out that life,
   That on earth could be neareſt to heaven,
Let him, thanking his ſtars, chooſe a wiſe,
   To whom truth and honour are given ;
But honour and truth are ſo rare,
   And horns, when they're cutting, ſo tingle,
That with all my reſpeƈt for the fair,
   I'd adviſe him to ſigh and live ſingle.

IV.

It appears from theſe premiſes plain,
   That wiſdom is nothing but folly,
That pleaſure's a term that means pain,
   And that joy is your true melancholy.
That all thoſe who laugh ought to cry,
   That 'tis fine friſk and fun to be grieving ;
And that ſince we muſt all of us die,
   We ſhould all be unhappy while living.

SONG LXXI.

WHEN YOUTH HIS FAERY REIGN BEGAN.

When youth his fae - ry reign be -

- gan; Ere for - row had pro - claim'd me man; While

peace the prefent hour be - guil'd, And all the lovely

pro - fpect fmil'd; Then, Ma - ry mid my light - fome

glee, I heav'd the figh I heav'd the pain - lefs figh for

thee, I heav'd the figh, I heav'd the pain - lefs figh for thee!

2

And when, along the waves of woe,
My harafs'd heart was doom'd to know
The frantic burft of outrage keen,
And the flow pang that gnaws unfeen;
Then fhipwreck'd on life's ftormy fea,
I heav'd an anguifh'd figh for thee.

3

But foon reflection's power impreft
A ftiller fadnefs on my breaft;
And fickly hope, with waning eye,
Was well content to droop and die;
I yielded to the ftern decree,
And heav'd a languid figh for thee!

4

And tho' in diftant climes to roam,
A wand'rer from my native home,
I fain would foothe the fenfe of care,
And lull to fleep the joys that were!
Thy image may not banifh'd be,
I heave a hopelefs figh for thee!

T

SONG LXXII.

IN MY PLEASANT NATIVE PLAINS,

Allegro.

In my pleafant na-tive plains, Wing'd with blifs each mo-ment flew; Nature there in-fpir'd the ftrains, Simple as the joys I knew: Jocund morn and ev-'ning gay, Claim'd the merry merry roun - de - lay, Claim'd the

merry merry rounde - lay.

Fields and flocks and fragrant flow'rs,
All that health and joy impart,
Call'd for artlefs mufic's pow'rs,
Faithful echoes to the heart.
Happy hours for ever gay,
Claim'd the merry roundelay.

But the breath of genial fpring,
Wak'd the warblers of the grove,
Who, fweet birds, that heard you fing,
Would not join the fong of love?
Your fweet notes and chauntings gay
Claim'd the merry roundelay.

SONG LXXIII.

FOR EVER FORTUNE.

JACKSON

For ever Fortune wilt thou prove, An un - re - lenting foe to love, And when we meet a mutual heart, Come in between and bid us part. Bid us figh on, from day to day, And wifh and wifh our souls away, 'Till youth and genial years are flown, and all the life of

life is gone.

II.

But bufy bufy ftill art thou,
To bind the lovelefs joylefs vow,
The heart from pleafure to delude,
And join the gentle with the rude.
For once, O Fortune, hear my pray'r,
And I abfolve thy future care,
All other bleffings I refign,
Make but the dear AMANDA mine.

WHILE I QUAFF THE ROSY WINE.

While I quaff the rofy wine, With en - liven'd wit I fhine, with en - li-ven'd wit I fhine; Singing then the mu - fe's praife, double fire in - fpires my lays, - - - - - - - - - - - - double fire in - - fpires my lays.

C O N T I N U E D:

II.

While I quaff the rofy wine,
I feel I feel the pow'r divine
Free me from all forrow's fway,
I puff like winds my care away.

III.

While I quaff the rofy wine, -
All my faculties refine :
My temper grows ferene and fair,
And like the Summer evening's air.

IV.

While I quaff the rofy wine,
Crowns of od'rous flow'rs I twine ;
Singing to the echoing grove,
The pleafures of that life I love.

V.

While I quaff the rofy wine,
To foft paffions I incline ;
My miftrefs then my fong employs,
And all love's pleafing painful joys.

VI.

While I quaff the rofy wine,
Every paft delight is mine,
Youth does again my veins infpire,
I lead the dance and join the choir.

VII.

While I quaff the rofy wine,
I its force to reafon join,
And fteel my breaft againft that fall,
The common fate that waits us all.

SONG LXXV.

THE WORDS BY CHARLES II.

P. HUMPHREY.

I pass all my hours in a shady old grove, But I
live not the day when I see not my love: I survey ev'ry
walk now my Phillis is gone, And sigh when I think we were
there all a - lone; O then 'tis O then that I think there's no
hell, like lo - - - - - ving too well.

But each fhade and each confcious bow'r, when I find,
Where I once have been happy, and fhe has been kind;
When I fee the print left of her fhape in the green,
And imagine the pleafures may yet come again;
    O then 'tis I think that no joys are above
      The pleafures of love.

While alone to myfelf I repeat all her charms,
She I love may be lockt in another man's arms,
She may laugh at my cares, and fo falfe fhe may be,
To fay all the kind things fhe before faid to me;
    O then 'tis O then that I think there's no hell
      Like loving too well.

But when I confider the truth of her heart,
Such an innocent paffion, fo kind without art,
I fear I have wrong'd her, and hope fhe may be
So full of true love to be jealous of me;
    And then 'tis I think that no joys are above
      The pleafures of love.

U.

SONG LXXVI.

KIND ROBIN LO'ES ME.

Come all ye souls devoid of art, Who take in virtue's cause a part, And give me joy of Robin's heart, For kind Robin lo'es me. O happy happy was the hour, and blest the dear delightful bow'r Where first I felt love's gentle pow'r, And knew that Robin

lo'ed me.

O witnefs ev'ry bank and brae,
Witnefs ye ftreams that thro' them play,
And ev'ry field and meadow gay,
　　That kind Robin lo'es me.

Tell it, ye birds! from ev'ry tree,
Breathe it, ye winds! o'er ilka lea,
Ye waves! proclaim from fea to fea,
　　That kind Robin lo'es me.

The winter's cot, the 'fummer's fhield,
The freezing fnaw, the flow'ry field,
Alike to me true pleafures yield,
　　Since kind Robin lo'es me.

For warld's gear I'll never pine,
Nor feek in gay attire to fhine;
A kingdom's mine if Robin's mine,
　　The lad that truely lo'es me.

SONG LXXVII.

SINCE EMMA CAUGHT.

TRAVERS.

Since Em - ma caught my ro - - ving eye, Since Em - ma

Since Emma caught my ro - ying eye, Since

fix'd my wav - ring wav - ring heart, I long to

Em - ma fix'd my wav - 'ring heart,

fmile, I fcorn to figh, But na - ture tri - umphs

I long to fmile, I fcorn to figh, But na - ture

tri umphs o - ver art. If fuch the hap -

tri - umphs o - ver art. If fuch

less mo - ments prove, Ah who would give his heart to

the hap - less mo - ments prove, Ah who would give his

love ? Ah who would give, would give his heart to love would

heart to love, his heart to love, would give his heart to

give his heart to love his heart to love? If such the

love, would give his heart to love, his heart to love?

hap - less mo - ments prove, Ah who would give ah who would

If such the haplefs mo - ments prove, Ah who would

give his heart to love ?

give - his heart to love?

SONG LXXVIII.

NOW WESTLIN WINDS.

REICHARDT.

Slow.

Now weftlin winds and flaughtring guns, Bring au - tumn's plea - fant

wea - ther, The moorcock fprings on whir - ring wings, A -

mang the bloom - ing hea - ther; Now waving grain wide

o'er the plain De - lights the wea - ry far - mer; And the

moon fhines bright as I rove at night To mufe u - pon my char - mer.

CONTINUED.

The Partridge loves the fruitful fells ;
  The Plover loves the mountains ;
The Woodcock haunts the lonely dells ;
  The foaring Hern the fountains ;
Thro' lofty groves the Cuſhat roves,
  The path of man to ſhun it ;
The hazel buſh o'erhangs the Thruſh,
  The ſpreading thorn the Linnet.

Thus ev'ry kind their pleaſure find,
  The ſavage and the tender ;
Some ſocial join and leagues combine ;
  Some ſolitary wander :
Avaunt, away ! the cruel ſway,
  Tyrannic man's dominion ;
The ſportſman's joy, the murd'ring cry
  The flutt'ring gory pinion !

But Peggy dear, the ev'ning's clear,
  Thick ſlies the ſkimming ſwallow ;
The ſky is blue, the fields in view,
  All fading green and yellow :
Come let us ſtray our gladſome way,
  And view the charms of nature ;
The ruſtling corn, the fruited thorn,
  And ev'ry happy creature.

We'll gently walk, and ſweetly talk,
  Till the ſilent moon ſhine clearly ;
I'll graſp thy waiſt, and, fondly preſt,
  Swear how I love thee dearly ;
Not vernal ſhow'rs to budding flow'rs,
  Not Autumn to the Farmer,
So dear can be as thou to me ,
  My fair, my lovely Charmer !

SONG LXXIX.

BENEATH THIS GREEN WILLOW.

SCHULZ.

Be - neath this green willow, My Phœbe's re - treat, The soft turf her seat, My bosom her pillow, What transports I knew! How blest the hours flew! Ah willow, Beneath this green willow.

But long tempest-tost,
Now Phœbe is lost
On life's stormy billow,
I sit all alone
And make my sad moan
  Ah willow !
Beneath this green willow.

SONG LXXX.

'TIS NOT WEALTH.

Giardini.

'Tis not wealth it

is not birth Can value to the foul con - - vey,

Minds pof - fefs fu - - pe rior worth, which chance nor.

X

gives nor takes a - - way, chance nor gives nor takes a -.

way - - - - - nor takes a - way.

Like the fun true merit fhows, By nature warm by

nature bright, with in - bred flames he no - bly glows with

in - bred   flames   he   nobly   glows,   nor needs   the

aid   of   borrow'd   light, nor needs the   aid of   borrow'd light.

X 2

SONG LXXXI.

FROM GRAVE LESSONS.

WELDON.

From grave leſſons and reſtraint, I'm ſtole out to revel here, Yet I tremble and I pant, in the middle of the fair. O O O wou'd fortune in my way throw a lover kind and gay, Now's the time, nows the time now'sthe time he ſoon may move, A young heart un - uſ'd to love.

Shall I venture no, no, no, shall I from the danger

go? O no, no, no, no, no, no, no, no, no, no, no, no, no, no,

no, I must not try, I cannot fly I must not dare not cannot

A - - - - - - y, I must not try, I cannot

fly, I must not dare not, cannot fly.

Help me na-ture Help me art, Why should I de-

ny my heart? Help me nature help me

art, Why should I de - -ny my heart?

If a lover will pur - sue, Like the

. wi - - sest let me do, I will fit him

if he's true, If he's false I'll fit him
too.

HASTE MY NANETTE.

TRAVERS.

Hafte - - my Nanette, my love-ly maid, Hafte -

Hafte - - my Nanette, my lovely maid,

- to the bow'r to the bow'r thy fwain thy fwain has made. For

Hafte - - to the bow'r to the bow'r thy fwain has made.

thee a-lone I made the bow'r, And ftrew'd the couch with many a flow'r for

For thee alone I made the bow'r, and ftrew'd the couch with

thee alone I made the bow'r, for thee for thee a-lone for thee for

many a flow'r for thee alone I made the bow'r for thee for thee alone for thee

thee alone I made I made the bow'r, for thee a-lone

- - alone I made - I made the bow'r for thee a-lone

I made the bow'r, and ftrew'd the couch with many a flow'r; for thee a

made the bow'r & ftrew'd the couch wt. many a flow'r for thee a- lone I made the

lone I made the bow'r and ftrd the couch wt. many a flow'r for thee a- lone I

bow'r, and ftr'd the couch wt. many a flow'r for thee a - lone I made - I

made the bow'r, and ftrew'd the couch with many a flow'r.

made the bow'r, and ftrew'd the couch with many a flow'r.

None but my fheep fhall near us come; Venus be prais'd my fheep are

None but my fheep fhall near us come, Venus be prais'd my

dumb, none, none but my fheep fhall near us come, none none but my fheep fhall

fheep are dumb, none none but my fheep fhall near us come, none none but my.

CONTINUED.

near us come; Venus be prais'd my ſheep are dumb, Venus be
ſheep ſhall near us come; Venus be prais'd my ſheep are dumb,
prais'd - - - - - , my ſheep my ſheep are dumb.
Venus be prais'd my ſheep my ſheep are dumb.
Slow.
Great God of love take thou my crook take thou my crook to keep
Great God of love take thou my crook to keep to
Soothingly.
to keep the wolf from Nanette's flock. Guard thou the ſheep to
keep the wolf from Nanette's flock. Guard thou the ſheep to
her ſo dear, My own a - las are leſs my care.
her ſo dear, My own a - las are leſs my care.

CONTINUED.

Soft. ... **Loud.**

But of the wolf if thou'rt a - fraid, Come not to us to afk for aid.

But of the wolf if thou'rt a - fraid, Come not to us to afk for aid,

With spirit.

For with her fwain my love fhall ftay, For with her fwain my love fhall ftay,

For with her fwain my love fhall ftay, For with her fwain my love fhall

Tho' the wolf ftroll, ... and the fheep ftray

ftay, Tho' the wolf ftroll - . . - . and the fheep ftray

For with her fwain my love fhall ftay, tho the wolf ftroll . . . .

For with her fwain my love fhall ftay tho the wolf ftroll . .

and the fheep ftray

and the fheep ftray

SONG LXXXIII.

IF THE TREASUR'D GOLD COULD GIVE.

REICHARDT.

If the treasur'd gold could give, Man a longer term to live,

If the treasur'd gold could give, Man a longer term to live

If the treasur'd gold could give, Man a longer term to live,

I'd em-ploy my ut-moſt care, Still to keep and ſtill to ſpare,

I'd em-ploy my ut-moſt care, Still to keep and ſtill to ſpare,

I-d em-ploy my ut-moſt care, Still to keep and ſtill to ſpare,

And when death ap-proach'd would ſay, Take thy fee and walk a-

And when death ap-proach'd would ſay, Take thy fee and walk a-

And when death ap-proach'd would ſay, Take thy fee and walk away, Take thy fee and walk a - way.

way, Take thy fee and walk a - way.

way, Take thy fee and walk a - way.

II.

But fince riches cannot fave,
Mortals fram the gloomy grave,
Why fhould I myfelf deceive,
Vainly figh and vainly grieve?
Death will furely oe my lot,
Whether I am rich or not.

III.

Give me freely while I live,
Generous wines in plenty give,
Soothing joys my life to cheer,
Beauty kind and friends fincere;
Happy could I ever find,
Friends fincere and beauty kind.

SONG LXXXIV.

BLOW YE BLEAK WINDS.

Blow ye bleak winds a-round my head, And footh my heart cor - - roding care;

Flafh round my brows ye lightnings red, And blaft the laurels planted there, But may the maid where-e'er fhe be,

Think not of my diftrefs nor me; But may the maid where-

e'er fhe be, Think not of my dif - trefs nor me,

Think not of my dif - trefs, nor me.

II.

May all the traces of our love,
Be ever blotted from her mind ;
May from her breaft my vows remove,
And no remembrance leave behind ;
But may the maid where e'er fhe be,
Think not of my diftrefs nor me.

III.

O ! may I ne'er behold her more ;
For fhe has robb'd my foul of reft :
Wifdom's affiftance is too poor,
To calm the tempeft in my breaft ;
But may the maid where-e'er fhe be,
Think not of my diftrefs nor me.

IV.

Come death, O ! come thou friendly fleet
And with my forrows lay me low :
And fhould the gentle virgin weep,
Nor fharp nor lafting be her woe ;
But may fhe think where-e'er fhe be,
No more of my diftrefs nor me.

GREEN GROW THE RASHES O.

There's nought but care on ev'ry hand, In ev'ry hour that passes O; What signifies the life o' man, An' twere not for the lasses O?

Green grow the rashes O; Green grow the rashes O; The

sweetest hours that e'er I spend, Are spent a-mang the lasses O;

The wardly race may riches chace
  An' riches still may flie them O;
An' tho' at last they catch them fast,
  Their hearts can ne'er enjoy them, O;
    Green grow &c.

Gie me a canny hour at e'en,
  My arms about my dearie, O;
An wardly care, an' wardly men,
  May a' gae tapsailteerie, O;
    Green grow, &c

For you sae douse ye snarl at this,
  Ye're nought but senseless asses O:
The wisest man the warld' e'er saw,
  He dearly loe'd the lasses O;
    Green grow, &c.

Auld nature swears, the lovely dears,
  Her noblest work she classes O,
Her prentice han' she try'd on man,
  An' then she made the lasses, O;
    Green grow, &c.

Z

SONG LXXXVI.

MY DAYS HAVE BEEN SO WONDROUS FREE.

My days have been so wond'rous free, The little birds that

fly, With carelefs eafe from tree to tree, Were but as bleft as

I. Afk gliding waters, if a tear Of mine increaf'd their

flowing ftream, Or afk the flying gales, if e'er I lent one

- figh to them.

II.

But now my former days retire,
  And I'm by beauty caught ;
The tender chains of sweet defire,
  Are fix'd upon my thought.
An eager hope within my breaft
  Does ev'ry anxious doubt controul,
And charming Celia ftands confeft
  The fav'rite of my foul.

III.

Ye nightingales, ye twifted pines,
  Ye fwains that haunt the grove,
Ye gentle echoes, breezy winds,
  Ye clofe retreats of love ;
With all of nature, all of art,
  Affift the foft and dear defign ;
O, teach a young unpractif'd heart
  To make fair Celia mine.

IV.

The very thought of change I hate,
  As much as of defpair ;
Nor ever covet to be great
  Unlefs it be for her.
'Tis true, the paffion in my mind
  Is mixt with a fevere diftrefs ;
Yet while the fair I love is kind,
  I cannot wifh it lefs.

TO ANACREON IN HEAVEN.

To A - na - creon in heav'n where he fat in full glee, A

few fons of harmony fent a petition, That he their infpirer and

patron would be ; When this anfwer ar - riv'd from the jolly old Grecian; Voice

fiddle and flute, no longer be mute, I'll lend you my name and in -

fpire you to boot, And be - fides I'll inftruct you like me to in - twine, The

myrtle of Venus with Bacchus's vine.

The news through Olympus immediately flew,
When Old Thunder pretended to give himself airs,
" If these mortals are suffer'd their scheme to pursue,
" The devil a goddess will stay above stairs.
" Hark ! already they cry, with transports of joy,
" Away to the sons of Anacreon we'll fly,
" And there with good fellows, we'll learn to intwine,
" The myrtle of Venus with Bacchus's vine."

" The yellow hair'd god and his nine fusty maids,
" From Helicon's banks will incontinent flee ;
" Idalia will boast but of tenantless shades,
" And the bi-forked hill a mere desart will be ;
" My thunder no fear on't, will soon do its errand,
" And dam'me I'll swinge the ringleaders I warrant,
" I'll trim the young dogs for thus daring to twine,
" The myrtle of Venus with Bacchus's vine."

Apollo rose up and said, " Prythee ne'er quarrel,
" Good king of the gods, with my vot'ries below ;
" Your thunder is useless ;" then shewing his laurel,
Cry'd, Sic evitabile fulmen, you know !
" Then over each head my laurels I'll spread,
" So my sons from your crackers no mischief shall dread,
" Whilst snug in their club-room, they jovially twine,
" The myrtle of Venus with Bacchus's vine."

Next Momus got up, with his risible phiz,
And swore with Apollo he'd chearfully join ;
" The full tide of harmony still shall be his,
" But the song, and the catch, and the laugh shall be mine,
" Then Jove be not jealous of these honest fellows."
Cry'd Jove, " We relent, since the truth you now tell us,
" And swear by old Styx, that they long shall intwine,
" The myrtle of Venus with Bacchus's vine."

Ye sons of Anacreon, then join hand in hand ;
Preserve unanimity, friendship, and love ;
'Tis your's to support what's so happily plann'd ;
You've the sanction of gods, and the fiat of Jove.
While thus we agree, our toast let it be,
" May our club flourish happy, united, and free,
" And long may the sons of Anacreon intwine,
" The myrtle of Venus with Bacchus's vine."

SONG LXXXVIII.

HOW PLEAS'D WITHIN MY NATIVE BOW'RS.

SHIELD.

Amoroso.

How pleaſ'd within my native bow'rs e'erwhile I paſs'd the

day, Was ever ſcene ſo deck'd with flowr's, were ever flow'rs ſo

gay? How ſweetly ſmil'd the hill, the vale, and all the landſcape

round, The ri - ver glid - ing down the vale, The

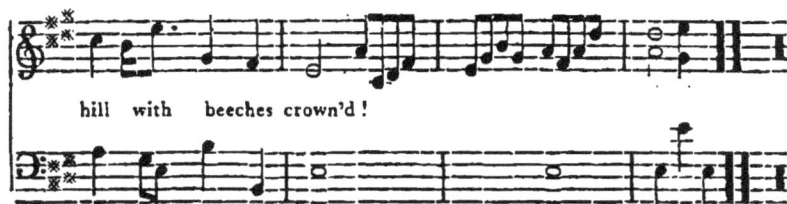

hill   with   beeches crown'd !

II.

But now when urg'd by tender woes,
    I speed to meet my dear,
That hill and stream my zeal oppose,
    And check my fond career.
No more since Daphne was my theme,
    Their wonted charms I see,
That verdant hill, and silver stream,
    Divide my love and me.

SONG LXXXIX.

ON ADMIRAL DUNCAN'S VICTORY.

En - roll'd in our bright annals lives Full many a gallant name, But never Britiſh heart conceiv'd A prouder deed of

crown, Than noble Duncan's mighty arm atchiev'd off Camper -

down. To fhield our li - ber - ties and laws, to guard our fov'reign's

crown, Im - mortal be the glorious deed at-chiev'd off Camperdown.

II,

October the eleventh it was, he fpied the Dutch at nine,
The Britifh fignal flew to break their clofe embattled line ;
Their line was broke, for all our tars on that aufpicious day
All bitter memory of the paft had vowed to wipe away.
Their line was broke &c,

III.

At three o'clock nine mighty fhips had ftruck their colours proud,
And two brave Admirals at his feet their vanquifhed flags had bowed :
Our Duncan's towering colours ftreamed all honour to the laft,
For in the battles fierceft rage, he nailed them to the maft ;
Our Duncan's towering colours &c.

IV.

The victory was now complete ; the cannon cea.'d to roar ;
The fcatter'd remnants of the foe flunk to their native fhore ;
No power the pride of conqueft had his heart to lead aftray,
He fummoned his triumphant crew, and thus was heard to fay,

Chorus. " Let every man now bend the knee, and here in folemn pray'r,
" Give thanks to GOD, who in this fight has made our caufe his care,

V.

Then on the deck, the noble field of that proud days renown,
Brave Duncan with his crew devout before their God knelt down,
And humbly blefs'd his Providence, and hail'd his guardian power,
Who valour, ftrength, and fkill infpir'd in that dread battle's hour.
And humbly blefs'd &c.

VI.

The captive Dutch this folemn fcene furvey'd with filent awe,
And rue'd the day when Holland join'd to France's impious law,
And marked, how virtue, courage, faith, unite to form this land,
For victory, for fame, and power, juft rule, and high command.
And marked &c.

VII.

The Venerable was the fhip, that bore his flag to fame,
Our veteran hero well becomes his gallant veffel's name ;
Behold his locks! they fpeak the toil of many a ftormy day;
For fifty years and more, my boys, has fighting been his way.

Grand Chorus.

Behold his locks! they fpeak the toil of many a ftormy day,
For fifty years and more my boys, has fighting been his way ;
The Venerable was the fhip that bore his flag to fame,
And Venerable ever be our vet'ran DUNCAN's name !

SONG XC.

WILT THOU BE MY DEARIE.

Wilt thou be my dear-ie; When forrow wrings thy gentle heart, O
wilt thou let me chear thee? By the treafure of my foul, That's the love I bear thee, I
fwear and vow, that only thou Shalt ev - er be my dearie.

Only thou I fwear and vow, fhall ev - er be my dearie.

Laffie, fay thou lo'es me,
Or if thou wilt na be my ain,
Say na thou'lt refufe me;
If it winna canna be,
Thou for thine may chufe me,
Let me laffie quickly die,
Trufting that thou lo'es me.

2 A 2

SONG XCI.

O YE IN YOUTH AND BEAUTY'S PRIDE.

SCHULZ.

O ye in youth and beauty's pride, Who light-ly dance a-

O ye in youth and beauty's pride, Who lightly dance a-

O ye in youth and beauty's pride, Who lightly dance a-

long, While laughter fro-licks at your side, And rapture tunes your

long, While laughter fro-licks at your side, And rapture tunes your

long, While laughter frolicks at your side, And rapture tunes your

song. What tho' each grace a-round you play, Each beauty bloom for

song. What tho' each grace a-round you play, Each beauty bloom for

song. What tho' each grace a-round you play, Each beauty bloom for you, Warm as the blush of ri - sing day, And sparkling

you, Warm as the blush of ri - sing day, And sparkling

you, Warm as the blush of ri - sing day, And sparkling

as the dew.

as the dew.

as the dew.

The blush that glows so gaily now,
But glows to disappear,
And quiv'ring from the bending bough,
Soon breaks the pearly tear!
So pass the beauties of your prime,
That e'en in blooming die;
So shrinking at the blast of time,
The treach'rous graces fly.

With charms that win beyond the sight,
And hold the willing heart,
O learn then to await their flight,
Nor sigh when they depart;
These graces shall remain behind,
These beauties still controul,
The graces of the polish'd mind,
The beauties of the soul.

SONG XCII.

SAPPHO'S HYMN TO VENUS.

O Ve - nus, beauty of the skies, To whom a thou - sand temp - les rise; Gay - ly false in gen - tle smiles, Full of love - per - plex - ing wiles, O God - dess from my heart re - move The wast - ing cares and pains of love.

If ever thou haft kindly heard
A song in foft diftrefs preferr'd;
Propitious to my tuneful vow,
O gentle Goddefs hear me now.
Defcend thou bright immortal gueft,
In all thy radiant charms confeft.

CONTINUED.

Thou once didſt leave almighty Jove,
And all the golden roofs above :
Thy car the wanton ſparrows drew,
Hov'ring in air they lightly flew;
As to my bower they wing'd their way,
I ſaw their quiv'ring pinions play.

The birds diſmiſt, while you remain,
Bore back their empty car again:
Then you, with looks divinely mild,
In ev'ry heav'nly feature ſmil'd,
And aſk'd what new complaints I made,
And why I call'd you to my aid;

What frenzy in my boſom raged,
And by what cure to be aſſwaged,
What gentle youth I would allure,
Whom in my artful toils ſecure;
" Who does thy tender heart ſubdue,
" Tell me, my Sappho, tell me who ?"

" Tho' now he ſhuns thy longing arms,
" He ſoon ſhall court thy ſlighted charms;
" Tho' now thy off'rings he deſpiſe,
" He ſoon to thee ſhall ſacrifice;
" Tho now he freeze he ſoon ſhall burn,
" And be thy victim in his turn,

Celeſtial viſitant, once more
Thy needful preſence I implore!
In pity, come and eaſe my grief,
Bring my diſtemper'd ſoul relief,
Favour thy ſuppliant's hidden fires,
And give me all my heart deſires.

SONG XCIII.

FOR TENDERNESS FORM'D.

For tendernefs form'd in life's early day, a parent's foft forrows to mine led the way, A

parent's foft forrows to mine led the way,

caught from her eye, And e'er words were my own, I spoke with a sigh.

II.

The nightingale plunder'd, the mate widow'd dove,
The warbled complaint of the suffering grove,
To youth as it ripen'd gave sentiment new,
The object still changing, the sympathy true.
Soft embers of passion, yet rest in the glow,
A warmth of more pain may this breast never know!
Or if too indulgent the blessing I claim,
Let the spark drop from reason that wakens the flame.

B b

ALL IN THE DOWNS.

All in the Downs the fleet was moor'd, The streamers

All in the Downs the fleet was moor'd, The streamers

wa - ving in the wind; When black-ey'd Su - san

wa - ving in the wind; When black-ey'd Su - san

came on board, "O where shall I my true love find?

came on board, "O where shall I my true love find?

Tell me ye jo - vial sai - lors tell me true, If my sweet Wil - liam

Tell me ye jo - vial sai - lors tell me true, If my sweet Wil - liam

if my sweet Wil - liam sail a - mong your crew?"

if my sweet Wil - liam sail - mong your crew?"

II.

William who high upon the yard,
Rock'd with the billows to and fro,
Soon as her well known voice he heard
He figh'd and caſt his eyes below:
The cord ſlides ſwiftly thro' his glowing hands,
And quick as lightning on the deck he ſtands.

III.

So the ſweet lark high poiſ'd in air,
Shuts cloſe his pinions to his breaſt,
(If chance his Mate's ſhrill call he hear)
And drops at once into her neſt.
The nobleſt Captain in the Britiſh Fleet,
Might envy William's lips thoſe kiſſes ſweet.

IV.

O Suſan, Suſan, lovely dear,
My vows ſhall ever true remain;
Let me kiſs off that falliug tear,
We only part to meet again,
Change as ye liſt, ye winds, my heart ſhall be
The faithful compaſs that ſtill points to thee.

V.

Believe not what the land men ſay,
Who tempt with doubts thy conſtant mind,
They'll tell thee, ſailors when away
In every port a miſtreſs find.
Yes, yes, believe them when they tell you ſo,
For thou art preſent whereſoe'er I go.

VI.

If to fair India's coaſt we ſail,
Thy eyes are ſeen in diamonds bright,
Thy breath is Africk's ſpicy gale,
Thy ſkin is ivory ſo white:
Thus ev'ry beauteous objeċt that I view,
Wakes in my ſoul ſome charms of lovely Sue.

VII.

Though battle calls me from thy arms,
Let not my pretty Suſan mourn;
Tho' canons roar, yet ſafe from harms,
William ſhall to his dear return.
Love turns aſide the balls that round me fly,
Leſt precious tears ſhould drop from Suſan's eye.

VIII.

The boatſwain gave the dreadful word,
The ſails their ſwelling boſom ſpread,
No longer muſt ſhe ſtay aboard:
They kiſs'd, ſhe ſigh'd, he hung his head.
Her leſs'ning boat, unwilling rows to land:
Adieu, ſhe cries, and wav'd her lily hand.

SONG XCV.

SOME WOMEN TAKE DELIGHT IN DRESS.

Some women take delight in drefs And fome in cards take pleafure; While others place their happi-nefs in hoarding heaps of treafure: Some like a fo-cial tete-à tete Their artlefs charms un-folding; But thefe miftake the fov'reign fete, There's no fuch joy as fcolding; But thefe miftake the fov'reign fete, There's no fuch joy as

scolding, There's no such joy as scolding.

2

The inftant that I ope mine eyes,
  Adieu all day to filence ;
Before my neighbours they can rife,
  They hear my tongue a mile hence.
When at the board I take my feat,
  'Tis one continued riot ;
I eat and fcold, and fcold and eat,
  My clack is ne'er at quiet.

3

Too fat, too lean, too hot, too cold ;
  I ever am complaining ;
Too frefh, too ftale, too young, too old,
  Each gueft at table paining :
Let it be fowl, or flefh, or fifh,
  Tho' of my own providing,
I ftill find fault with ev'ry difh,
  Still ev'ry fervant chiding.

4

But when I go to bed at night,
  I furely fall to weeping ;
For then I lofe my great delight ;
  Oh could I fcold when fleeping !
But this my pain doth mitigate,
  And foon difperfes forrow,—
Altho' to-night it be too late,
  I'll pay it off to-morrow !

I AM A POOR SHEPHERD UNDONE.

I am a poor shepherd un - done, And cannot be cu - red by

art ; For a nymph, as bright as the sun Has stole a - way my

heart. And how to get it a - gain, There's

none but she can tell To cure me of my pain By

saying she loves me well, And a - las poor shepherd, a - lack and a-well-a-

day Be - fore I was in love oh ! e - ve - ry month was May.

She afk'd me of my eftate ;
  I told her a flock of fheep ;
The grafs whereon they graze,
  Where fhe and I might fleep ;
Befides a good ten pound,
  In old king Harry's groats,
With hooks and crooks abound
  And birds of fundry notes.
And alas &c.

If to love fhe fhould not incline,
  I told her I'd die in an hour.
To die, fays,fhe, 'tis in thine ;
  But to love, 'tis not in my pow'r.
I afk'd her the reafon why
  She could not of me approve ;
She faid 'twas a tafk too hard
  To give any reafon for love.
And alas &c.

ROY'S WIFE OF ALDIVALLOCH.

Roy's wife of Al - di - valloch Roy's wife of Al - di - valloch

Wat ye how she cheated me as I came o'er the braes of Balloch?

She vow'd she swore she would be mine; She said she lo'ed me best of o - ny But

ah the fause the fic - kle quean She's ta'en the Carle & left her John - nie.

Her hair's sae fair, her een's sae clear,
Her wee bit mou's sae sweet and bonny,
To me she ever will be dear,
Tho' she's for ever left her Johnnie.
   Roy's wife &c.

But O, she was the canty quean.
And weel could dance the highland walloch,
How happy I had she been mine,
Or I'd been Roy of Aldivalloch!
   Roy's wife &c.

THE LOVER HOW BLEST.

Slow. SCHULZ.

The lo-ver how bleſt! For him all the charms by kind Nature diſ-play'd, Re-flect but the charms of his favour-ite maid; The lover how bleſt, the lover how bleſt!

The lover how bleſt!
He hears in the carol that burſts from the grove
The voice of his fair-one confeſsing her love ;
The lover how bleſt, the lover how bleſt !

The lover how bleſt !
The ſoft-flowing ſtreams as they gurgle impart
The whiſper of love and the throb of the heart ; &c.

The lover how bleſt !
The dew-drops that bend while they deck the ſweet flower,
Are the tear-ſwimming eye, In affection's ſoft hour ; &c.

The lover how bleſt !
The bluſh of the dawn leading on chearful day
Is the cheek of his love ſmiling ſorrow away ; &c.

The lover how bleſt !
The evening in dun ſober mantle array'd
Reſembles the virtues that deck his chaſte maid, &c.
The lover how bleſt, the lover how bleſt.

2 C

SONG XCIX.

VAIN IS EVERY FOND ENDEAVOUR,

ARNE:

Vain is ev·'ry fond en - deavour

to re - fift the tender dart ; For ex - amples move us never,

We muft feel to know the fmart: When the fhepherd

fwears he's dying, And our beauties fets to view : Va - ni - ty her aid   ſupply - ing, Bids us think 'tis all our due, Bids us think 'tis

all our due.

Softer than the vernal breezes, ·
 Is the mild deceitful ſtrain ;
Frowning truth our ſex diſpleaſes,
 Flatt'ry never ſues in vain ;
Soon, too ſoon, the happy lover,
 Does our tend'reſt hopes deceive ;
Man was form'd to be a rover,
 Fooliſh woman to believe.

SONG C.

COME LET'S BE MERRY.

Come let's be merry, let's be ai - - ry, 'Tis a folly

to be fad, For fince the world's grown mad, mad mad,

Why fhou'd we a - lone be wife, And like dull

fools, and like dull fools and like dull fools gaze on

other men's joys.

Let not to-morrow bring your forrow,
While the ftream of time flows on,
But when the blifsful day is paft,
Still endeavour that the next
Be full as gay, and as little perplex'd.

If you have leifure, follow pleafures
Let not an hour of blifs pafs by ;
For as the fleeting moments fly,
Time it will your youth decay,
Then ftrive to live, and bo bleft whilft you may.

If you have plenty, nought will torment you,
But yet your felves, your felves may annoy ;
Hearty and free's the poor man's joy ;
Gladly yielding the minutes pafs,
And when old Time fhakes him, takes off his glafs.

SONG CI.

HOW STANDS THE GLASS AROUND.

HANDEL.

How ſtands the glaſs a - round? For ſhame ye take no care, my boys, How

How ſtands the glaſs around? For ſhame ye take no care, my boys,

ſtands the glaſs a - round? Let mirth and wine a - bound: The

How ſtands the glaſs around? Let mirth and wine a - bound: The

trumpets ſound, the colours they are fly - ing, boys, To

trumpets ſound, the colours they are fly - ing, boys, To

fight, kill or wound; May we ſtill be found, Con - tent with our hard

fight, kill or wound; May we ſtill be found, Con - tent with our hard

fate, my boys, on the cold ground.

fate, my boys, on the cold ground.

II.

Why, Soldiers, why,
Shou'd we be melancholy boys?
Why Soldiers, why,
Whofe bufnefs 'tis to die !
What, fighing, fie !
Damn fear, drink on, be jolly boys,
'Tis he, you or I,
Cold, hot, wet, or dry ;
We're always bound to follow, boys,
And fcorn to fly.

III.

'Tis but in vain,
I mean not to upbraid you, boys,
'Tis but in vain
For Soldiers to complain ;
Shou'd next campaign
Send us to him who made us, boys,
We're free from pain !
But if we remain,
A bottle and kind landlady
Cure all again.

SONG CII.

GOLDEN SKIES.

SHIELD.

The night when fpent in golden fkies, If whiten'd cliffs the failor

fpies the failor fpies compleatly bleft the fight each tender thought in-

fpires his love's on fhore, And fancy fires and fancy fires his faithful

breaft the dancing waves falute his oar, He pulls and fings my love's on fhore, He pulls and fings My love's on fhore.

He waves his hat, and cries " Adieu,
" Farewell good fhip and loving crew,
" Farewell good fhip; for love I fteer."
And as around he turns his face,
To view the happy well known place,
The happy place that holds his dear,
The dancing waves falute his oar,
He pulls and fings, " My love's on fhore,"
He pulls and fings, " My love's on fhore,"

SONG CIII.

LITTLE THINKS THE TOWNSMAN'S WIFE.

Little thinks the town's-man's wife, While at home she tar - ries,

What must be the lass - 's life Who a sol - dier mar - ries;

Now with weary marching spent, Dancing now be - fore the tent;

Li - ra li - ra la, li - ra li - ra la, With her jol - ly

fol - - - dier.

2

In the camp at night she lies,
Wind and weather scorning;
Only griev'd her Love must rise,
And quit her in the morning;
But the doubtful skirmish done,
Blithe she sings at set of sun,
Lira lira la, Lira lira la,
With her jolly soldier.

3

Should the Captain of her dear
Use his vain endeavour,
Whisp'ring nonsense in her ear,
Two fond hearts to sever;
At his passion she will scoff,
Laughing thus she'll put him off;
Lira lira la, Lira lira la,
For her jolly soldier.

LOVE'S A TRIFLING SILLY PASSION.

Love's a trifling fil - - - - ly paffion, Often teafing

fel - dom pleafing; If we're conftant, if we're conftant fure to

cloy; Love's a tri - - fling fil - ly paffion, Often teazing

Seldom pleafing; If we're conftant fure to cloy -

- - - - - - - If we're

conſtant ſure to cloy. Let us follow inclination; Always

ranging Ever changing, Brings a freſh ſupply of joy, - -

- - - - - Brings a

freſh ſup - ply of joy.

SONG CV.

O WHERE HAVE YE BEEN A' DAY.

O where have ye been a' day, my boy Tammy? Where have ye been a' day, my boy Tam - my ? I've been by burn and flow'ry brae, Meadow green, and mountain grey, Courting o' this young thing juſt come frae her Mammy.

And where gat ye that young thing? my boy Tammy.
I gat her down in yonder howe,
Smiling on a broomy knowe,
Herding a wee lamb and ewe for her poor Mammy.

What ſaid ye to that young thing? my boy Tammy.
I praiſ'd her een fae lovely blue,
Her dimpled cheek and cherry mou ;
I pree'd it aft, as ye may true, ſhe ſaid ſhe'd tell her Mammy

I held her to my beating heart; " My young, my fmiling Lammy,
" I hae a houfe, it coft me dear,
" I've walth o' plenifhin and geer,
" Ye'fe get it a' war't ten times mair, gin ye will leave your Mammy.

The fmile gade aff her bonny face; " I manna leave my Mammy ;
" She's gi'en me meat, fhe's gi'en me claife,
" She's been my comfort a' my days,
" My father's death brought mony waes ; I canna leave my Mammy."

" We'll tak her hame and mak her fain, my ain kind hearted Lammy,
" We'll gie her meat ; we'll gie her claife;
" We'll be her comfort a' her days ;"
The wee thing gi'es her hand and fays, " There ! gang and afk my Mammy

Has fhe been to kirk wi' thee ? my boy Tammy,
She has been to kirk wi' me,
And the tear was in her ee,
But oh ! fhe's but a young thing, juft come frae her Mammy !

SONG CVI.

DUNCAN'S WARNING.

RECITATIVE.

As o'er the heath, amid his fleel-clad Thanes,
  The royal Duncan rode in martial pride,
Where, full to view, high topp'd with glitt'ring vanes,
  Macbeth's ftrong tow'rs o'er-hung the mountain's fide:
In dufky mantle wrapp'd, a grifly form
  Rufh'd with a giant ftride acrofs the way;
And thus, while howl'd around the rifing ftorm,
  In hollow thund'ring accents pour'd difmay.

Stop, O King, thy def - tin'd courfe, Furl thy ftandard, turn thy
horfe; Death be - fets this on - ward track, Come no
fur - ther, quickly back.

Hear'ft thou not the raven's croak?
See'ft thou not the blafted oak?
Feel'ft thou not the loaded fky?
Read thy danger, king, and fly.

Lo! yon caſtle banners glare
Bloody thro' the troubled air,
Lo! what ſpectres on the roof,
Frowning bid thee ſtand aloof.

Murder, like an eagle, waits
Perch'd above the gloomy gates,
Juſt in act to pounce his prey,
Come not near — away, away.

Let not plighted faith beguile
Honour's ſemblance, beauty's ſmile;
Fierce ambition's venom'd dart
Rankles in the feſt'ring heart.

Treaſon, arm'd againſt thy life,
Points his dagger, whets his knife,
Drugs his ſtupifying bowl,
Steels his unrelenting ſoul.

Now 'tis time; ere griſly night
Cloſes round thee, ſpeed thy flight;
If the threſhold once be croſt,
Duncan, thou'rt for ever loſt.

On he goes! reſiſtleſs fate
Haſtes to fill his mortal date:
Ceaſe, ye warnings! vain tho' true,
Murder'd king, adieu! adieu!

SONG CVII.

I AM, SAID APOLLO.

am cry'd A - pollo, when Daphne he woo'd, And panting for

breath the coy virgin pursu'd, When his wisdom in manner most

am - ple ex - prest, The long list of graces his

godfhip poffeft, When his wif - dom in manner moft

ample expreft The long lift of graces his

godfhip poffeft.

II.

" I'm the god of fweet fong and infpirer of lays."
Nor for lays nor fweet fong the fair fugitive ftays.
" I'm the god of the harp—ftop my faireft." In vain;
Nor the harp nor the harper could bring her again.

III.

" Ev'ry plant, ev'ry flow'r, and their virtues I know ;
" God of light I'm above, and of physic below."
At the dreadful word physic, the nymph fled more fast,
At the fatal word physic, she doubled her haste.

IV.

Thou fond god of wisdom, then, alter thy phrase;
Bid her view thy young bloom, and thy ravishing rays ;
Tell her less of thy knowledge, and more of thy charms,
And, my life for't, the damsel will fly to thy arms.

COME MY PRETTY LOVE.

Come my pretty love, Let us hafte away, Freely let us rove,

Come my pretty love, Let us hafte away, Freely let us rove,

Where the lambkins play, Where the painted lawn, deckt wt. op'ning flowrs

Where the lambkins play, Where the painted lawn, deckt wt, op'ning flowrs

To the glowing morn, Balmy incenfe pours.

To the glowing morn, Balmy incenfe pours.

Sweet the rofes blow, fweet the tedded hay,
Sweet the heifers low, round the dewy lee ;
Hark ! the feather'd train chant their fongs with glee,
Oh ! the fprightly ftrain! come my love with me.

Not the dawn of day, not the breath of herds,
Not the lambkins play, nor the fong of birds,
Not the blufhing rofe, nor the tedded hay,
Can one charm difclofe, when my love's away.

SONG CIX.

HANG, MY LYRE, UPON THE WILLOW.

Hang, my lyre, upon the willow, Sigh to winds thy notes forlorn,

Or a - long the foaming billow, Float the wrecking

tempests scorn. Sprightly sounds no more it raises, Such as Laura's

smiles approve, Lau - ra scorns her poet's praises,

Calls his artless friendship love.

Calls it love, that spurning duty,
Spurning nature's chastest ties,
Mocks thy tears, dejected beauty,
Sports at fallen virtue's sighs.

Call it love, no more profaning,
Truth with dark suspicion's wound:
Or, my fair, the term retaining,
Change the sense, preserve the sound.

Yes, 'tis love, that name is given,
Angels to your purest flames,
Such a love as merits heaven
Heav'n's divinest image claims.

SONG CX.

THE MILKMAID. A Cantata.

RECITATIVE.

As Kate one morn, with milk-pail on her head,
Was trudging homeward thro' the verdant mead;
Her mind revolving on ten thousand ways
To fix a lover and her fortune raise;
Bright hope at once beam'd on her flutt'ring breast,
And as she went she thus herself address'd:

Sup - pose my milk sold some eggs I will buy, And chickens to raise di -

rectly I'll try, My poultry when rear'd will fetch a good price And two little

lambs I'll get in a trice, My flock will in - crease if for - tune but

smile Farewell then farewell then to labour and toil My flock will en -

creafe if fortune but fmile, Farewell then farewell then to labour & toil. Now

lovers a-round me will buz like a bee, No girl in our vi'lage fo

courted as me; But ruftics! a-dieu, no fuch conquefts I prize, the hearts I once

fought I now can despise; A lord or fome fquire my riches may win, And

titles and coaches are furely no fin; A lord or fome fquire my riches may

F f

win, And titles and coaches are surely no sin.

REC. Struck with the fancied bliss, Kate leapt for joy,
Ah! fickle fortune! why her hopes deftroy?
Down came the pail, and in the mighty fall,
Eggs, chickens, lambs, lords, fquires, are vaniſh'd all!

Fair ladies who my tale attend, forgive this mo-ral from a friend like

ruin'd Kate pray be not catcht nor count your chicks before theyre hatcht, nor

count your chicks be-fore they're hatcht nor count your chicks before they're hatcht nor count your chicks be-fore they're hatcht your chicks before they're

hatcht yonr chicks be - fore they're hatcht, your chicks before they're

hatcht. Fair ladies who my tale attend, Forgive this mo - ral

from a friend, Like ruin'd Kate pray be not catcht, nor count, your

chicks be - fore they're hatcht Like ruin'd Kate pray be not catcht nor

F f 2

count your chicks be - fore they're hatcht nor count your chicks before they're

hatcht, nor count your chicks be - fore theyre hatcht; nor count your

chicks your chicks be-fore they're hatcht, yonr chicks be - fore they're

hatcht, your chicks before they're hatcht.

SONG CXI.

TASTE LIFE'S GLAD MOMENTS.

Taſte life's glad moments whilſt the waſting ta - per glows,

Pluck e're it wither the quickly fad - ing roſe.

Man blindly follows grief and care, He ſeeks for thorns and

finds his ſhare, whilſt violets to the deſert air un -

heeded ſhed their bloom. DA CAPO.

WHEN NICHOLAS FIRST TO COURT BEGAN.

When Ni - cho - las first to court be - gan, And Blanch approv'd his

When Ni - cho - las first to court be - gan, And Blanch approv'd his

When Ni - cho - las first to court be - gan, And Blanch approv'd his

love, U - nited time and pleasure ran, Like turtles in the grove.

love, U - nited time and pleasure ran, Like turtles in the grove.

love, U - nited time and pleasure ran, Like turtles in the grove.

In joy and sweet de - light, They pass'd each day and night When

In joy and sweet de - light, They pass'd each day and night, When

In joy and sweet de - light, They pass'd each night wh

Ni - cho - las firft to court be - gan, And Blanch approv'd his

Ni - cho - las firft to court be - gan And Blanch approv'd his

Nicho - las firft to court be - gan Aud Blanch approv'd his

love. Happy and gay, Smiling as May, Jo - cund they

love, Happy and gay, Smiling as May, Jocund they

love. Happy and gay, Smiling as May, Jocund they

pafs'd each day and night.

pafs'd each day and night.

pafs'd each day and night.

When children bleſt the loving pair,
   Kind Heav'n incread'd their ſtore,
Their boys were brave, their girls were fair,
   And each a portion bore,
Of rural induſtry,
With dance and ſong and glee,
   Happy and gay &c.

Tho' age their heads with ſilver crown'd.
   Affection did increaſe,
Diſſention ne'er their hearts could wound,
   Nor jealouſy their peace ;
And ſtill remembrance ſweet,
Their placid minds would greet.
   Happy and gay &c-

MY JO JANET.

Sweet Sir, for your courtesy, When ye come by the Bafs, then, For the love ye bear to me, Buy me a keeking glafs, then; Keek into the draw-well Ja - net, Janet, And there ye'll fee your bonny fell, My jo; Janet.

Keeking in the draw-well clear,
   What if I fhou'd fa' in, Sir?
Then a' my kin will fay and fwear
   I drown'd myfell for fin, Sir.
Had the better by the brae, Janet, Janet;
Had the better by the brae, My jo, Janet

Kind Sir, for your courtefy,
   Coming thro' Aberdeen, then,
For the love ye bear to me,
   Buy me a pair of fheen, then.
Clout the auld the new are dear, Janet, Janet,
Ae pair may gain ye half·a year, My jo, Janet.

But what if dancing on on the green,
   And fkipping like a maukin,
Folk fhou'd fee my clouted fheen,
   Of me they will be talking;
Dance ay laigh, and late at e'en, Jaret, Janet,
Syne a' their fau'ts will no be feen, My jo, Janet.

THE COTTAGE BOY.

Morn shakes her locks, the budding rose Smiles at the part - ing

twilight grey, In re - no - vat - ed beauty blows, And sheds her perfume

on the day, In re - novated beauty glows & sheds her perfume on the

day; When Lubin, nature's rustic child, Tries calm contentment to en-

joy, And sweetly in his wood- notes wild, thus chearful sings the

Cottage boy, thus chearful fings, thus chearful fings

thus chearful fings the Cottage boy.

How bleft my days fince Sylvia's kind!
    No other joy I wifh to know,
For in her fmiles foft blifs I find,
    In her all gentle virtues glow;
The flaves of fortune let me fhun,
    My humble cottage to enjoy,
When toil and labour's o'er and done,
    Thus chearful fung the Cottage Boy.

Returning at mild ev'ning's hour,
    Perhaps my Sylvia I may meet,
For her I'll pull the chiceft flower,
    And ftrew it at my fair one's feet.
Then as it drooping dies 'twill prove,
    That time e'en beauty will deftroy,
How tranfient then is youthful Love!
    Thus chearful fung the Cottage Boy.

SONG CXV.

AT DEAD OF NIGHT.

At dead of night when care gives place, In other

breasts to soft re - pose, My throb - bing heart feel

no re cess, Since love and Chloe are my foes: At

morn when Phœbus from the East, re - pels the gloomy

breaſt, Redoubles at th' approach of day,

At noon when moſt intenſe he ſhines,
My ſorrows more intense are grown;
At ev'ning, when the ſun declines,
They ſet not with the ſetting ſun.

To my relief then haſten death!
And eaſe me of my reſtleſs woes;
With joy I will reſign my breath,
Since love and Chloe are my foes.

SONG CXVI.

ADIEU THE VERDANT LAWNS AND BOW'RS.

A - dieu the verdant lawns and bow'rs, A - dieu my peace is

A - dieu the verdant lawns and bow'rs, A - dieu my peace is

o'er, A - dieu the sweetest shrubs and flow'rs since Delia breathes no

o'er, A - dieu the sweetest shrubs and flow'rs since Delia breathes no

more, A - dieu ye hills a - dieu ye vales, A - dieu ye streams and

more, A - dieu ye hills a - dieu ye vales, A - dieu ye streams and

floods, A - dieu sweet echo's plaintive tales, A - dieu ye meads and

floods, A - - dieu sweet echo's plaintive tales, A - dieu ye meads and

woods, a - dieu ye flocks ye fleecy care, a - dieu yon pleasing

woods, a - dieu ye flocks ye fleecy care, a - dieu yon pleasing

CONTINUED.

plain,   A - dieu   thou beaut'ous   blooming   fair   we

plain,   a - dieu   thou beaut'ous   blooming   fair   we

ne'er fhall   meet a - gain.

ne'er fhall meet   a - gain.

SONG CXVII.

HEY HOE TO THE GREENWOOD.

Hey hoe to the greenwood now let us go sing heave and hoe, And

Hey hoe to the greenwood now let us go sing heave

Hey hoe to the greenwood now

there shall we find both buck & doe sing heave & hoe the hart & hind,& the little pret_

and hoe & there shall we find both buck & doe sing heave & hoe the

let us go sing heave and hoe and there shall we find bt buck & doe sing heave &

ty roe sing heave and hoe. Hey hoe to the greenwood now

hart & hind & the little pretty roe sing heave and hoe, Hey hoe.

and hoe ye hart & hind & ye little pretty roe sing heave & hoe.

www.ingramcontent.com/pod-product-compliance
Lightning Source LLC
Chambersburg PA
CBHW020852270326
41923CB00006B/662

* 9 7 8 3 3 3 7 1 2 6 3 4 6 *